THE CLASSROOM AS COSMOS

Teaching as Pattern Application

DAVID MATHWIN

ACKNOWLEDGMENTS

I have benefited greatly from having wonderful students whose curiosity and work ethic far outstripped my own when I was their age. They all deserve a great deal of credit for these pages. The stories I include happened, but I have altered them in certain small ways, including changing the names of the students involved.

My thanks to the many wonderful teachers I have worked with and learned from over the years, and to the bosses who have encouraged and tolerated my various antics and experiments.

Around 2017–18 I discovered Jonathan Pageau and his *Symbolic World* podcast. This book would not exist without his work. I will cite him when I can, but his influence oozes out of these pages. He in turn led me to St. Maximus the Confessor, St. Ephrem the Syrian, and Matthieu Pageau's *The Language of Creation*, among others.

My thanks also to my primary editors. Kim Bookless has a razor for a mind and corrected hundreds of grammar and style errors. Maria Copeland is a colleague and a great young teacher in her own right. Some of these chapters owe much to her advice. Hudson Hadley and Kaelan Wilburn are former students, and I was greatly honored that they both read this book in advance. They also had their influence on the final shape of its contents. But all errors that remain in the text are mine alone.

Finally, to my wife, Linda, and my children, John, AJ, and Keris. What words can I say?

CONTENTS

PREFACE

I began teaching in 1998 at Ad Fontes Academy (AFA) partially by accident. I originally thought of entering pastoral ministry after grad school. When that obviously looked like a bad idea, I fell back on the family trade. My father taught for more than thirty-five years at Montgomery Blair High School, and my mom taught various grades for many years in different contexts, as well as serving in an administrative role later in her career. I had the great good fortune of being able to pick their brain many times over the years.

The late '90s were something of the Wild West in the Classical Christian world. This meant I had little structure or scaffolding from which to work, and this certainly led to me making some big mistakes and wrong turns. But it also meant I entered on the ground floor and had opportunities to try many different things.. Though I mostly teach history, I have also taught classes in rhetoric, PE, literature, Bible, contemporary culture, and film. I have also coached guys and girls basketball and worked (badly) as the athletic director for a few years. For the last twelve years, I have also served as AFA's dean of students in addition to my teaching load. This has allowed me to participate in discussions about which teachers we should hire, who we should let go, and so on. Mainly, however, my dean of students role has allowed me to have several hundred conversations over the years with my students, getting their thoughts on teachers, homework, and student life. These have been both quite helpful and enormously enriching in aiding my understanding of the teaching profession.

INTRODUCTION

I cannot stand teacher movies. The idea of teachers as heroes, as inspirational, as molding and shaping, and so on—this has never appealed to me. *Dead Poets Society*? Ugh. No teacher should have the influence that Robin Williams's character had over his students. And he did it all with Walt Whitman's "unlock your true self" ickiness no less? Bleah. *Saturday Night Live*'s parody of the final "O Captain, my Captain," scene remains to this day the only good thing to come from that movie.[1]

So this book will not seek to "inspire" the reader.

A variety of solid books already exist about teaching. They tend to fall into two distinct categories:

1. Memoirs with some good stories and helpful specificity, where the author finds that—wait for it—the students have actually taught *him* more than he taught the students.

2. Books that give one a good framework for teaching, with certain maxims to follow in a general way.

Certainly, one can read these books and benefit from them.

I find that such books lack two things, one minor, the other more substantial.

The minor omission involves not talking about teaching as a job that requires a certain approach and certain skills. Society tends to romanticize teachers as underpaid martyrs. Prospective or actual

---

1 Definitely worth five minutes of your time if you don't mind a lot of fake blood: https://www.youtube.com/watch?v=Ie6LpKOJVf0.

teachers should never indulge in such thoughts. Most teachers work hard. Some work in difficult circumstances. None make a lot of money. But teachers also get a lot of time off. They won't have to work weekends, and they will make their kid's soccer games. In addition, a lot of meaning comes built into their jobs. Teachers get burned out but rarely do they question their purpose in life. Understand the trade-offs, and understand that teaching is fundamentally a *job*, a job that requires a certain skill set—a prosaic truth but true nonetheless. Do not expect more of it than it can deliver.

The major omission involves providing a theological framework from which a teacher can approach their subjects and their students. The best teaching involves an unfolding, a revealing, of reality.[2] But students cannot take in reality all at once. How we unpack what we want to impart should not be arbitrary, because we experience the world in patterns. Understanding these patterns, then, will give teachers a crucial means to understand their role.

When students reflect on their favorite teachers, they often will say something along the lines of "Mr. Johnson didn't just teach me science/literature/music, he taught me about life." This overwrought cliché actually has something to it. I would guess Mr. Johnson probably rarely stopped science class to talk about "life." Instead, he probably had a way of teaching his subject that seemed poetic. A proper way of revealing even something small can connect with us deeply, and we intuitively recognize that this process brings us into a deeper awareness of life itself. Science, literature, and math can all serve as a fractal that can lead us to such deeper patterns embedded in creation.

I have taught for more than twenty-five years, almost entirely at the junior high and high school level. Like most teachers, I have

---

2   By "reality," I mean to include religious and moral truths, beauty, and the like.

had bumps and bruises along the way, many of them self-inflicted, especially early on. In general, I have had success in the profession, but when asked for advice by others, I struggled to explain how to learn from what they observed me doing. Now, I believe I have more understanding of the teacher's role that can translate to others. I define the basic premise of this book as:

Teaching involves an unfolding of universal, biblical patterns within specific contexts.

This book should give you insight into how to do just that.

The best teachers unfold their subjects intuitively. But teaching is not all art. In this book, I hope to show readers some of the patterns in creation. Understanding this framework can help teachers have more awareness of how and why certain classroom approaches work and why others, despite the best intentions, fail. However, I make no claim to present a foolproof plan or a step-by-step how-to guide. Every teacher needs to experiment and find their way through trial and error. I hope that this book will shorten the time spent in error and increase one's sense of enjoyment and success in the profession.

This book also seeks to re-enchant you with teaching or introduce it to you in a way you might not have considered. It will not answer every question or make teaching easy. I still second-guess myself and make mistakes. This book explains to you patterns ground in reality, which will give you a true framework to inhabit. This will make decisions easier to make, and you will have more confidence in those decisions. Part I of this book will lay out the basics of this framework, and Part II will give guidance on how to apply these patterns in your classroom.

A full disclosure about myself is in order.

I have taught the entirety of my career with a Classical-Christian curricular method, and this obviously has shaped me. I appreciate the classical method, but other good approaches exist as well. No one philosophy has cornered the market. What I hope to elucidate in the book has an application in public, private, or homeschooling contexts.

Many thanks to all who will continue and take the plunge, and welcome to your classroom, a cosmos all its own.

PART I

The Patterns
of Creation

CHAPTER 1

Decisions, Decisions

Imagine, if you will, the following scene, which happened some years ago.

Class has dismissed and the students cram the halls. I immediately notice Gus, Bill, and Steve, three eighth-grade friends, at the far end of the hall. As they walk to their next class, they play a form of human billiards. Gus slams into Bill, whose momentum carries him into Steve, who flies into the wall beside him. Steve then starts the process over, lowering his shoulder into Bill, who careens into Gus.

They laugh loudly and enjoy themselves. For my part, I enjoy watching them. But . . . they can't act this way, right? I think about saying something. Then, Gus inadvertently knocks into Sally, a tiny seventh-grade girl, dashing her notebook on the floor. Sally, annoyed but unhurt, picks up her notebook and moves quickly past them. Now I will definitely say something.

"Gentlemen!" I bark.

No response. Not a flicker. Their radar cannot pick up such signals.

"Gus, Bill, Steve!" They stop now and look up at me. Gus and Steve blink rapidly, as if I just woke them out of a nap.

"Uhhh . . . sir? Uhhh . . . yes?"

"Gentlemen, what are you doing?" I instantly regret this question—not direct enough.

Their brows furrow. *What were we doing?* they seem to be thinking. And again with the rapid blinking.

I tell them what I saw and then add, "And what about Sally?"

Another pointless question. I should have known better. They dart their eyes at each other. Gus furrows his brow and silently mouths to Steve, "Sally?" Of course, as a seventh grader, Sally exists in an alternate universe closed to mere mortals such as they. I decide to wrap this up, as class will start soon. "No pushing each other. No roughhousing in the hallway. Understood?"

"Uh . . . yes, yes sir."

We move off in our opposite directions. After a few steps, however, I turn back around. Sure enough, the three amigos have started all over again, albeit in a less aggressive way.

"Gentlemen!" I bark again. This time they stop and respond— amazing improvement!

"Uh, yes, what? Sir? I, um . . ."

"Gentlemen, please remember. Just because *you* can't see *me* doesn't mean that *I* can't see *you*."

Total puzzlement on their faces, their eyes now wide open. Gus seems to mouth to Bill, "How *can* he see . . . if we can't . . ." Steve's face says, "He's joking . . . I think." But now, chastened and definitely perplexed, they walk to their class as more or less normal human beings.

Such encounters happen all the time in every school, but a moment's reflection reveals one of the challenges teachers face: the need to make several decisions within a few moments. If you handle the situation badly, you could end up in the principal's office just as easily as a student. This minor incident involves the following queries:

1. Should I punish them for their behavior?

2. When they started up again after I talked with them the first time, were they ignoring me or just clueless?

3. Should I make them apologize to Sally?

4. Would Sally want an apology, or does she just want to move on with her day? Would it be worth it to grab her out of class and hold up the guys from their class to apologize? Would that make life harder for Sally that day?

5. Does it matter or not if Sally wants the hassle, and the apology, if apologizing is the right thing in this case?

One quickly realizes in the example above that an absolute law would not work (i.e., "Anytime anyone shoves someone, they lose their recess," or something like that). You could not find refuge in the opposite corner either (i.e., "Just pay attention to the particular facts of a particular situation."). This approach leaves the question of which particular facts have weight, which don't, and how we make those judgments.

This mundane incident serves as an illustration of what teachers face. Indeed, a variety of studies exist that show teachers make more decisions per day than even top surgeons.[3] This inevitable need to

---

3   See https://www.edweek.org/teaching-learning/1-500-decisions-a-day-at-least-how-teachers-cope-with-a-dizzying-array-of-questions/2021/12 as just one example.

make (at minimum) several hundred decisions per day not only tires teachers out but can sap their confidence. Of course, we can reflect on our actions, but teachers have no time and no ability to reflect on everything. In any case, reflection can only help you after the fact. In the moment, you need the right instincts for quick, calm, decisive action.

So, then, how can we make decisions?

Education in even the best schools removes teachers and students alike from the flow of ordinary life. Most of the great sages we revere and learn from never started school at 8:00 a.m., moving to different classes every forty-five minutes or so, ending at 3:00, with thirty minutes for lunch, and so on. No wonder students often feel that school has no point in itself, though some will value school as an end to . . . more school. We cannot ultimately avoid the industrial regimentation of school life, but we must understand that our artificial environments fail to give students meaning and coherence.

In fact, the standard pattern of a school day works against comprehension of meaning. It brings us into a kind of chaos where we lose our bearings. It should not surprise us that our students engage in much aimless mental (and sometimes physical) wandering.

Faced with this reality, many teachers feel, I believe, that they have two choices:

1. Make things up as you go with no particular framework to guide decisions, or

2. Have a framework from which to act, but you don't really believe in the framework. You made it up, or your boss made it up, or some think tank made it up. Either way, this frame has no more meaning than your English class lasting forty-five instead of forty-eight

minutes, so you won't really believe in it, and you won't have confidence in acting from it. At best, what you have is only convenient. At worst, you feel like a fraud.

Whether you pick option 1 or 2, you end up confused and exhausted. A lot of teachers burn out after a few years for this very reason. We know working with students has great importance. This must be true, right? Then why can it often feel so stale?

I believe teachers can at times be their own worst enemy, reinforcing the artificiality inherent in the school environment. Certainly, every job has its own drudgery, and everyone has their bad days. But if we pay attention to how God made the world, and how Christ incarnates these patterns, we have every hope of getting ahead of the curve. We will begin by seeing how God orders space and time.

Space and Time

One day years ago after lunch, I walked into my sixth-period class a few minutes early. There sits Brenda, a bright senior. She looks less than thrilled for class to start.

"So, Brenda," I begin, noticing her gloomy expression, "things can't be that bad, can they?"

"I just got to eat food and hang out with friends, and now . . . you know . . . class . . . *this*." She spreads out her hands over the empty classroom as she says "this."

I play along. "I would think that because you just had lunch, you might have hit the reset button, so to speak, for more of *this*." I spread my hands out too.

She shakes her head disdainfully.

"So does the period before lunch work for you?" I inquire.

"Nope, because then during class you just think about lunch coming up."

"What about right at the start of the day then?"

"No way. I'm just waking up."

"Obviously, the end of the day . . ."

"After lunch it all runs downhill, Mr. Mathwin, and don't even talk about last period."

"Right. Teachers don't like last period either."

"I can tell."

"Right. So, Brenda, what period of the day hits your wheelhouse?"

After thinking, she admitted that perhaps during third period (ca. 9:30–10:30), teachers got "peak Brenda." Third period hit the sweet spot. She had woken up sufficiently, and it wasn't too close to lunch. But other than that, the day involved (a) shaking off sleep, (b) waiting for lunch, or (c) waiting to go home.

Brenda was a good student, and a great young lady. Perhaps she exaggerated a bit but probably not too much. Most students would concur. One might respond to Brenda that (1) life is tough and involves hard things, so get over it, and (2) back in my day, I had it much harder. You pampered younglings would never understand!

Students, by the way, love it when adults say things like this.

If we step back and go deeper, we see Brenda had a keen intuition. Charles Taylor noted in *A Secular Age* that one of the key distinctives of the modern age involves the homogenization of space and time.[4] Electricity gives hypothetical equality to all moments in a day. Our creation of the minute and the second allows us to impose a control of movement across vast reaches of space. But, like Icarus, we flew too close to the sun. Our drive to create a panoply of order and uniformity have led to great confusion for our society and, consequently, in our schools. Our experience of time and space now

____

4   See especially the first chapter of that work, "The Bulwarks of Belief."

has little overlap with how God actually made the world. Our daily lives in school resemble a jumbled state of chaos from which we can derive no meaning or purpose.

How this happens, and how we can rectify this problem, will be the subject of what follows. We cannot escape the times in which we live, but we can bend them back a bit toward reality and improve our classroom experience. Understanding how space and time function will provide a good foundation for this endeavor.

First we will examine the pattern of how God made the world.

CHAPTER 3

What Is Beauty?

Many years ago I taught a class in medieval history, and toward the end of the year we examined Renaissance art. In discussing such masters as Michelangelo and Raphael, the subject of beauty naturally arose. Students discussed the Renaissance and medieval eras, with some preferring medieval art and most others works from the Renaissance. I then attempted to pivot the conversation.

"So does this mean, then, that beauty has an objective quality?" Most of the students disagreed. Beauty, for them, remained subjective. I expected this answer and had a riposte ready.

"But you are comparing one thing to another and evaluating them. You declare one era's work superior to the other. Surely, you must have some standard in mind to aid your judgment."

The students mulled this over. Most wanted to push back against the objective nature of beauty and so thought perhaps they picked

Renaissance over medieval art because it looked more familiar to them. In other words, they realized on some level that they had been culturally trained to react more positively to Renaissance art. This comment intrigued me, as it has the potential for wisdom, but I pressed further.

"Does this mean that no one's preference can be called superior to the preference of another?" As I expected, they agreed with this statement.[5] After a few more comments, I continued to what I thought was my obvious (though perhaps extreme) clincher. "So imagine you have two people from two different cultures. They look at two different objects, (1) Victoria Falls and (2) a pile of severed heads. One claims Victoria Falls has the greater beauty, the other, the severed heads. Can we state that one of them is right and the other wrong?"

I expected the students to see that of course we could make this claim, and from there we would get to a place where we could begin to see the eternal, "true" nature of beauty itself. To my shock, only three or four students thought we could deem either judgment superior, or more true, than the other. If some had cultural training to think severed heads had more beauty, we could not say they erred. I admit, I had no idea where to go from there. I froze up. The discussion petered out.

Perhaps such statements should not have surprised me, even coming from those raised in Christian homes. Tremendous confusion exists today regarding the nature of beauty. While this book will not attempt to defend a general theory of beauty, I feel confident in saying that beauty comes from God, and beauty's incarnation

---

5   Embedded within this discussion lay a discussion about morality, which I bypass above. The students admitted morality was objective, at least in certain ways, but would not make the same case for beauty.

involves, among other things, a proper relationship involving form and function, and time and space.

If we think of a piece of beautiful music, for example, we would notice:

- A proper relationship to space, meaning the proper spacing of notes (i.e., rhythm).

- A proper relationship to time, meaning the music has proper change and variation, and a proper cycle of the themes and motifs in the music.[6]

- A proper context (i.e., the right space and time for the music). For example, an opera aria and a folk song might both contain the above elements, but we would not call both beautiful equally in every context.[7]

Creating beauty sometimes involves a great deal of hard work. At other times, however, we feel carried along by the current, and the words, notes, or brushstrokes flow from us easily. We know that in our encounters with beauty, it often hits us instantaneously, getting under our skin in moments. We then abide under its spell.

When we think of beauty in teaching, educators often talk of reading great literature, or having good paintings on the walls, or classical music playing as students work quietly. These ideas all have merit, but I would like to go further. Many teachers think a great deal about "what" to teach. I would like us also to consider "how" we

---

6   One of my editors suggested instead that rhythm belongs to the category of time, as the spacing of notes involves their distance to one another in time. Then perhaps tone and dynamics would belong to the category of space. This is a very interesting suggestion, one that I will have to contemplate. For now, at least, I will stick with the above formulation.

7   Here perhaps is some guidance into the subjective nature of beauty. Beauty has subjective elements, of course, but these subjective elements are subordinate to the "higher" objective components.

teach, and "when" to teach the "what." To do so, we need an introduction to biblical concepts of space and time.

Christians have debated how to interpret the Genesis creation narrative for a long time. Some see a literal account of how God made the world, while others tend toward a more poetic or metaphoric interpretation. I want to bypass typical debates on these questions here for a few different reasons. For one, definitively answering them would require much more space and knowledge than I possess. For another, I think such debates wrongheaded in approach.

Ancient creation narratives, as many have noted, do not seek primarily to tell us the physical facts about the world from a scientific perspective but rather how to perceive meaning and thereby act within the world.[8] To act with wisdom presupposes understanding, and this, I propose, is a key purpose of the early chapters of Genesis (though not their only purpose). My focus here involves how Genesis arms its readers for the task of apprehending meaning, fact, and activity within creation.

In Genesis 1:1–2, we notice a few key details immediately:

- "The Earth was formless and void," but

- "The Spirit of God hovered above the waters."

Like many ancient creation narratives, Genesis introduces the theme of chaos. When chaos prevails, we lose the ability to make distinctions between things. Everything gets shoved together in incomprehensible ways. Death can come to us quite easily in chaos, and not just physical death but also the death of meaning and purpose. One can lead to another. In many ancient conceptions of

---

8   Jordan Peterson's *Maps of Meaning* has a good discussion of this, especially the chapter "Three Levels of Analysis." He appears to have borrowed from some of Mircea Eliade's framework in doing so. St. Ephrem the Syrian's *Hymns on Paradise* develops some of these concepts in a much more directly Christian manner.

the world, water embodies chaos. Water, after all, brings everything together in unnatural ways. For example, if you have ever cleaned up after a flood, you often come upon random piles of stuff left after the water receded. And in the middle of large bodies of water, one easily loses their bearings. One wave looks just like another, and without land in sight, we have no means to orient ourselves and therefore no ability to act with purpose and intention.

But Genesis also immediately lets us know that the Spirit of God hovers above the waters. God has the situation in hand, so to speak.[9]

God then begins to make distinctions between things. Chaos may not be bad in itself—it poses no problem for God anyway—but we cannot live in chaos. Indeed, God Himself is the fullness of everything, and "no man can see [God] and live" (Ex. 33:20). God then prepares the world for Man by making distinctions between things, such as light and dark, morning and evening, the sea and dry land, and male and female. These distinctions are not arbitrary. Genesis gives us the proper lens from which to view the world and ultimately come to know God through our experience in creation. As Romans 1 indicates, when we operate within the created order correctly, we see God, and when we stray, we lose sight not just of creation but God Himself.

Armed with this basic understanding, we can examine the beauty of the pattern God gave us in creation.

---

9   The reader may think of Jesus's miracles involving water (i.e., stopping the storm, and walking on water) as in part references back to Genesis 1.

CHAPTER 4

Core, Fringe, and Chaos

I mentioned in the preface the significant debt I owe to Jonathan Pageau, whose work has taught me a great deal about symbolism, patterns, and biblical interpretation. Pageau works as an icon carver and speaker and also edits the *Orthodox Arts Journal* and *The Symbolic World* website and podcasts.[10] His work, in turn, led me to other similar thinkers, such as his brother Matthieu Pageau, Derek Fielder, and Jordan Peterson, as well as many of the patristic thinkers from which they draw inspiration, such as St. Gregory of Nyssa, St. Ephrem the Syrian, and especially St. Maximus the Confessor. I mention this because I want to give credit where due and have no wish to claim certain insights as my own. However, because of the fluid nature of their dialogue, and because almost all of their content is oral rather than written, I cannot cite specific chapter and verse

---

10   https://thesymbolicworld.com/ and https://orthodoxartsjournal.org/.

where I learned such concepts. I encourage you to check out their work.

For our purposes here, I will focus on two particular insights, developed by Pageau and drawn largely from St. Maximus's *On the Ecclesiastical Mystagogy*. Here St. Maximus draws a variety of connections between the structure of the body and the structure of the church building. He writes:

> *Now that blessed old man [St. Dionysius] used to say that at the first level of contemplation holy Church bears the imprint and image of God since it has the same activity as He does by imitation and in figure. For God, as the creator of all things, . . . makes them converge in each other by the singular force of his relationship to them as origin. Through this force he leads all beings to a common and unconfused identity of movement and existence, no one being originally in revolt against any other or separated from him . . .*
>
> *This reality abolishes and dims their particular relations concerning each other's nature, but not destroying them or removing their distinctions. Rather God does so by transcending their natures and revealing their natures more fully, as the whole reveals its parts. And just as the sun in its splendor outshines the stars both in nature and in energy, just as the parts come from the whole.*
>
> *It is in this way that the holy Church of God will be shown to be working for us the same effects as God, just as the image reflects the archetype. For a numerous and infinite variety of men and women exist throughout the world, but all can be born into the Church and through her all are recreated in the Spirit.*

The holy Church is an image of God because it realizes the same union of the faithful with God. As different as they are by language, places, and customs, they are made one in it through faith. God realizes this union among diverse natures without confusing them, but lessening and bringing together their distinction in a relationship with Himself as cause, principle, and end.

. . . Moreover, [St. Dionysius] used to say that God's holy church in itself is a symbol of the world as such, since it possesses the divine sanctuary as heaven and the beauty of the nave as earth. Likewise, the world is a church since it possesses heaven corresponding to a sanctuary, and for a nave it has the adornment of the earth.

. . . And again, from another point of view, holy Church is like a man, for the soul it has the divine altar, and for the body it has the nave [i.e., the part of the church where people sit]. It is thus the image and likeness of man who is created in the image and likeness of God.

Pageau, in turn, shows how the design of the temple, both in the Old Testament and in the Book of Revelation, have a similar structure.[11] A connection exists between God and man's existence, and everyday life, and we can see this structure play out in what Pageau terms "fractals."[12] That is, one has the "meta" pattern of the trinitarian life of God, which flows down into our own lives, which we also see in worship and daily life. To help explain this, we can take the Resurrection, of which fractals abound everywhere, such as in:

---

11   https://www.youtube.com/watch?v=lT5fao-5fCI.

12   https://www.youtube.com/watch?v=Ln2JgjNHe74.

- The planting of a seed in the ground that rises to bear fruit and give life

- Jonah going into the sea to rise again

- One goes to sleep and then awakes refreshed

We could go on, but understanding just this specific pattern gives enormous insight into even our most mundane tasks. For example, why say grace before meals? Well, we should express thanks for our food, but eating also participates in this death to life motif. We drop dead things into our mouths, which descend, and then, these very same dead things give us life. In a sense, when we say grace, we ask for a resurrection miracle. Why should we make our beds? Ultimately, because we believe in the resurrection, we believe in living as God lives, which means bringing order out of the chaos of death.[13]

After some time ruminating on how these patterns revealed themselves in the world, it struck me that teachers who could recognize how the rhythm of creation revealed itself in the classroom could greatly enhance their learning environments. One important pattern Pageau elucidates is that of the tripartite structure of what he terms the core, the fringe, and chaos. Others might use the term "order" instead of "core," with the same intended meaning.

I will go into greater detail in later chapters, but I will define them each here as they relate to how God made the world.

The core is the formation of light out of darkness, or dry land, or stable space, out of the waters of chaos. The core gives a place from which to act, a means of orientation. The distinctions God creates

---

13 Granted, this explanation might not *always* work. Many years ago I tried it on my ten-year-old and got a blank look. I then pivoted to "Because I said so" as the reason why he should make his bed. Alas, neither approach has any guarantee of success!

between various elements of creation allow us to perceive the world in manageable parts. We cannot take in everything all at once.

A good core provides crucial benefits, but the core is never meant as an end in itself. Think of a good household, with a loving and responsible mother and father. They will invest a lot in their children in the early years, with the intent that as they grow, their children will have the skills and confidence to leave the world of the parents to form their own core somewhere else. Thus, the world regenerates itself, just as a seed drops into the earth.

Compared to the core, chaos sounds evil, and indeed, often it brings destruction. But we need to pause, for change is not bad in itself, anymore than time (which brings change) is evil.

But if all we have is core and chaos, that would be like driving with only red and green lights. We need the yellow light to serve as a buffer between the two. Sometimes yellow means we speed up; other times we slow down. A proper fringe prevents swinging wildly between extremes. We can explore outside the core akin to dipping our toes in the water, easing into a changing environment.

I will go into more detail later in each of these areas. For now, you can likely glimpse how the overall structure of creation can fractally break down into other areas of experience, such as a home or even a classroom. But before we scale down too far, we'll take a cue from Plato's *The Republic* and examine how the core looks in a scale writ large, that of a civilization.

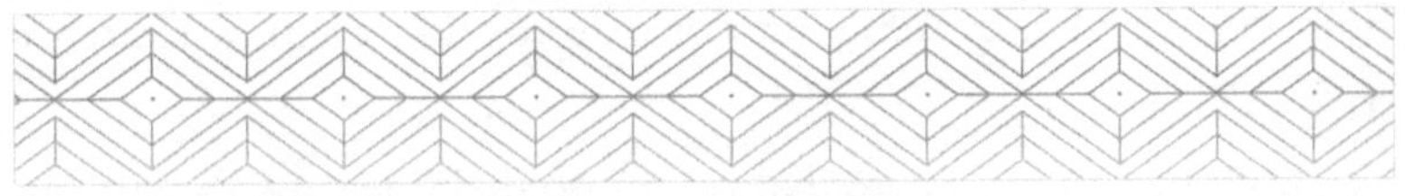

CHAPTER 5

The Core

The phrase "You can't see past the nose on your face," certainly applies to teachers at times. We rarely consider all the oddities school involves. For example, a solid majority of our students dislike school and would rather find themselves most anywhere else. Yet they eventually arrive without a great deal of fuss and then more or less willingly sit for several classes and go through the routine of the day. A few may create difficulties on occasion, but all in all, teachers benefit a great deal from the momentum of expectations about school in our society.

Such is the power of the core. It works even when sometimes it shouldn't.

In the ancient world, dry land often symbolized solidity and predictability. Thus, we can see God bringing "the firmament out of the midst of the water" (Gen 1:6) as the creation of order out of chaos, and God parting the Red Sea as Him bringing the Israelites from death to life as something of a re-creation event, a reference back to Genesis 1.

Each person has a core that makes up their identity. Parents can recognize in their kids the same habits, the same facial expressions, from eighteen months up to eighteen years and beyond. Every civilization by default must have a core of some kind that defines them. Even America, with its diversity and rapid cultural change, still has distinctive elements recognized anywhere, such as the summer blockbuster, blue jeans, and loud, fast cars.

As mentioned, groups with well-defined and large cores create an enormous amount of built-in momentum. With one's feet on the ground, so to speak, we "know where we stand." We understand our place, our role, and our purpose, and thus we can withstand enormous pressure and change around us.

If one looks at ancient Egypt, for example, one sees this principle play itself out in history. Situated within the Nile River valley, Egypt lived on some of the best soil in the ancient world. But on either side of this thin band of fertile ground lay the chaos of the desert. The distance between "life" and "death" may have been only ten to twenty yards in some places.[14] No doubt this influenced Egypt's concept of "Ma'at," the balance and tension between forces of order and chaos, and fixed them in place, from a cultural perspective.[15]

---

14   One can see this stark contrast in many images of the Nile River valley, such as here: https://smartours.com/wp-content/uploads/2019/05/nile_river_hero_iStock-960857756-e1556730437890.jpg.

15   For example, note how little their artistic style changes over thousands of years. An example of art from the Old Kingdom (https://i.pinimg.com/originals/63/dd/b1/63ddb1432e33df2d620643aacfa6ef15.jpg) and New Kingdom (https://farm1.staticflickr.com/202/504820000_fdd9fb15da_b.jpg) show very little difference.

We can admire Egypt for its longevity, continuity, and resulting stability.[16] Even its most famous structures, the pyramids, have lasted longer than any other ancient wonder of the world. But we should understand that such monuments have lasted as essentially massive weights of stone pressing down on the earth. Egypt's strong and well-defined core gave them the blessings of stability and the curse of immobility. When they had the chance to repent and come to know God, their hearts hardened. Their core turned to stone, and Egypt lost a chance at redemption.

This shows us an important truth. The categories of space (stability/core) and time (change/chaos) exist as descriptive and not moral elements of creation. Whether or not they serve as a blessing or curse to a person, a classroom, or a civilization depends on context.

Next we will explore the role of chaos.

---

16   Many of the same observations one could make about ancient Egypt in this regard would also apply similarly to ancient Chinese civilization.

CHAPTER 6

Chaos Rules

In the entry for AD 793, the *Anglo-Saxon Chronicle* relates, "immense whirlwinds and flashes of lightning, and fiery dragons . . . manifested over Northumbria and greatly terrified the people."

When reading such a text, moderns usually react in one of two ways:

1. "This shows how dumb medieval people were, because dragons never existed."

2. "Wow, I've been wrong all along. Dragons did exist, as the text reports."

It must be true, of course, that dragons either existed in a physically observable way that "literally" matches their description, or they did not. In this sense, the typical reactions of moderns mentioned above makes sense. However, we rarely take into account an additional layer of meaning in such texts. Whether or not they ever encountered a literal fire-breathing flying lizard may not have been even the main point ancient and medieval writers sought to make.

If we think about dragons as described by ancient texts, they make no sense. They are heavy, enormous creatures, yet they fly. They live solitary lives, not in community. They have no friends, only enemies. They live in the wilderness. One cannot integrate a dragon into normal life. Dragons bring chaos because they are themselves chaotic in their physical makeup and their actions. We must consider the possibility that the author of the *Anglo-Saxon Chronicle* meant to relate, in a manner familiar to his culture, that everything went upside down in AD 793.[17]

Because we cannot get our bearings when we encounter chaos, we cannot act appropriately, as we have no method of determining meaning. So erratic and dangerous behavior often follows our encounters with chaos.

Every teacher knows that the last day of school before a major break poses the biggest challenge. The students' bodies reside in school, but their minds lay elsewhere. Knowing this, teachers rarely want to schedule anything of academic importance. This generous act, however, only sends further signals to students that for today, at least, school has no purpose and thus no meaning. Beware the chaotic realm.

Perhaps the most dangerous day of the year might be the last day of school before Christmas vacation. I recall one such day years ago shortly after I had been named dean of students. Things started

---

17   Some translations insert the word "Vikings" instead of dragons, perhaps as an attempt to cover a perceived mistake of the author. This is foolish. Even if dragons never existed as we think, this kind of fix will not help us enter into the mind of the period.

calmly enough, but by fourth period, we had several seventh graders in the office for various offenses that seem to have piled up all at once. Tears flowed from more than one of them.

Investigation revealed that the students began the day with a party and plenty of sugar during first period. But then, in second period, they had a science quiz. After third period, they had a gift exchange planned, and apparently the rules for the exchange changed during second period, and so on.

The jumbled chaos of the day had clearly overwhelmed the students. We decided not to discipline anyone and sent the crying students home early for vacation.

This struck me as right then and now because we had contributed to the mess. Our failure to plan properly led the students into a chaotic realm where they had no firm guidelines and expectations about an unusual day in the calendar. We first said, "Have a party! Eat sugar!" Then, "Sober up! Take an important quiz!" Then, "Gifts for everyone! But hold on . . . not as we first agreed a week ago but in a different way that just now changed."

"Hic sunt dracones" (Here be dragons), whose presence naturally led to a social breakdown within the class. At least this unfortunate incident led to much better planning of such days moving forward. Times such as these need a lot more care and coordination than any regular school day.

We see the destructive pattern of chaos in the early chapters of Genesis. Cain's murder of Abel breaks down family order (among other things). Cain's punishment of wandering in the wilderness (chaos) mirrors his own actions. And then, Cain's experience of chaos in turn leads to violence in his descendants (Gen. 4:23–24). In Genesis 6:1–4, the improper mixing of the "sons of God" with the "daughters of men" brought about improper fruit, and violence followed.[18] One might suggest that such evil "called forth," in a sense, the chaos of the flood.

You might brush this aside. *Everyone has a bad day now and then, you think. But my students don't act violently against one another. You exaggerate.*

This misses my meaning. Chaos comes in different forms, and sometimes teachers can unwittingly call it forth. For example:

Many years ago I taught two classes of PE, one of them to second and third graders. Like most PE teachers, I sought to get the kids moving and having a good time. Occasionally I spiced it up a bit, and one week I decided to have a soccer Olympics of sorts. I divided the class into three teams and tallied up the points for several different events over a few class periods. I didn't want the students to focus too much on the points, however, and so rarely announced any of the standings. But on the last event of the last day, I noticed that the scores were in fact extremely close. Only a few points separated the Gold from the Bronze team. Everything, in fact, hinged on the last kick from the last guy in line for Team Three, Tommy.

I quieted everyone down. "Listen, everyone! It all comes down to this one moment, this one kick." The class got eerily quiet. "If Tommy makes this goal, Team Three wins the Gold!" Team Three cheered with gusto. "If he misses, Team Two wins the Gold!" Team Two would not be outdone by Team Three, and bellowed heartily. "Tommy, it's all on your shoulders! Give it your best shot! Let's hear it for Tommy!"

---

18   Most early interpreters see "sons of God" as meaning "fallen angels" of some kind. Others see the "sons of God" as the line of Seth and the "daughters of men" as the line of Cain. I strongly prefer the first option, but either way, the principle remains the same. Improper mixing led to chaos.

Tommy now looked white as a sheet, his eyes bulging from their sockets. His body tensed up, and he gave a yell as he ran up to kick the ball . . . which missed by about six inches to the left.

Instant cheers from Team Two, instant tears from Tommy, and some groans from Team Three. Looking back, I can easily see this as entirely my fault. I had ushered in chaos. I went from, "Let's have fun running around kicking a ball," and swerved massively to "Okay, the last thirty seconds of a nonchalant two-day event have suddenly gotten very serious, and it all rests on one kick from an eight-year-old."

At the time, I think I told Tommy to buck up, it was just a game, etc. How unfair to him! I had given the class the "just a game" message and then radically changed it at the last moment, then told Tommy that he should not have followed me in taking it so seriously.[19]

Of course, after this, I had to send the class back to their regular teacher, with some of them wondering what happened, some happy, some others mad, and . . . one kid in tears.

Good job by me.

Danger always attends chaos, but chaos in itself has regenerative possibilities, managed rightly. Scripture gives us various examples of this. In Genesis 1, we see the surprising detail that each day starts with night, with the sun going down, with the phrase, "It was evening, then morning," bracketing the first six days of creation. Certainly night brings a kind of chaos, for without light we cannot make distinctions between things, and so we cannot act rightly within such

---

19   For older students. this same principle applies. Sometimes teachers will play a game to review for a quiz. We often signal to them to relax, enjoy the game, and then sometimes the students can relax more than we expected. The temptation might be to try and tighten up, but again, if they follow your signal to relax, you can't punish them for relaxing a bit more than you expected. It will not work and will not win you any goodwill. Stick with your initial tone and ride it out.

environments. John in his gospel tells us that "if a man walk in the night, he stumbles," (11:10) and also that when Judas betrayed Jesus, "it was night" (13:30).

But note too that phenomenologically that as the sun goes into the earth, it gets "remade" for the next day. Sleep simply comes upon us, and we lose our bodies, in a sense, in sleep. Hence, sleep has always been viewed as a kind of death. But from death can come life. We should see a deep, patterned connection when Matthew tells us that God revealed the Incarnation itself to Joseph in a dream (1:18) and that God rescued the Wise Men from death to life in a dream (2:12). Ultimately, of course, God made both the night and the day, which are alike in his eyes (Ps. 139:12).

Some may balk at my linking of God with chaos. Certainly at times, chaos and order oppose each other. But the darkness and "chaos" in Genesis 1:2 stand not as an entity apart from God that God must somehow master but as an extension of His being. One may recall Mr. Beaver in *The Lion, the Witch and the Wardrobe* answering Susan's query about Aslan being "safe." "Safe? Who said anything about safe? Of course he isn't safe. But he's good. He's the King."

Indeed, God comes to upset order and remake it all at the same time. Sometimes chaos and order nearly shake hands. One can think of the Cross, both the worst and best thing that has happened. One can recall the healing brought by the serpent on the staff, a union of the straight and crooked (Num. 21, John 3:14). And we note that the greatest sign is that of Jonah (Mt. 12:38–45), the man who went down into death and remade the world.

God in His power and wisdom contains all things and can use all things for good, and teachers attuned to this pattern can take small steps in this direction.

CHAPTER 7

The Fringe

Many profound thinkers, and a great many rich mythologies, explore the interplay between chaos and order. When one looks at creation, various dualities reveal themselves, such as night and day or life and death. Some modes of Eastern thought explore the interplay between yin and yang.

Delving into these dualities can reveal much about our world. But a third category of space exists, revealed in Scripture, creation, and our everyday experience, a place that Jonathan Pageau (and others) have called the "fringe."[20]

The fringe exists as an indeterminate area of space, so describing it brings some difficulty. We can start with a sociological phenomenon, that of the disappearing front porch. No doubt you have had

---

20   I credit much of what follows to Pageau's insights, developed in his revelatory article about Pentecost and St. Christopher (https://orthodoxartsjournal.org/pentecost-for-the-zombie-apocalypse/) and in other podcasts and videos.

the experience of a salesman visiting your house. You want to be polite, and perhaps have an interest in their product. Inviting them into the house seems like too much too fast, but talking outside the house gets awkward quickly. A front porch solves that problem, serving as a bridge between the inner sanctum of the home and the great beyond.[21]

Or consider twilight, that sliver of time between the afternoon and evening, and those moments at morning and night when we lie neither quite awake or asleep.

God instructed Adam to work the garden, and in this way Adam was to be like God, forming the unformed. Proper work creates proper delineation, bringing boundaries and an appropriate degree of control over our environment. But we must limit our control. And we see that God leaves a part of the week, the seventh day, as a day of no work, a day where we create less order and make fewer distinctions. Interestingly, this day has no "evening, then morning," pattern to tie it off in the text. It lacks the normal boundaries of the other six days.

Pageau mentions some other key pointers to the reality of the fringe:

1. When the Israelites weave their garments, they are to
   leave tassels at their edges (Num. 15:38, Dt. 22:12).
   Weaving garments involves creating unity out of
   disparate matter, but in this case, the Israelites need
   to leave some material unworked.

---

21 Regarding the benefits of this in-between space, some may recall this snippet from Ray Bradbury's *Fahrenheit 451*: "No front porches. My uncle says there used to be front porches. And people sat there sometimes at night, talking when they wanted to talk, rocking, and not talking when they didn't want to talk. Sometimes they just sat there and thought about things, turned things over. My uncle says the architects got rid of the front porches because they didn't look well. But my uncle says that was merely rationalizing it; the real reason, hidden underneath, might be they didn't want people sitting like that, doing nothing, rocking, talking; that was the wrong KIND of social life. People talked too much. And they had time to think. So they ran off with the porches."

2. The Israelites need to leave the edge of their fields unharvested, to leave it wild in a sense (Lev. 23:22, etc.).

We should not see these laws as arbitrary, or as mere signaling devices of their difference from other cultures. Rather, God called His people to live into the pattern of the world He made directly and concretely. The example regarding their fields is very instructive—i.e., leave the edge of your fields as a "fringe" so that the fringe (the poor) of society have provision. Furthermore, the poor come to your property, and you will have to interact with them.[22] Interacting with the "other" brings fear for most, but we know from experience how it can transform us.

God gives us a fringe built into creation, and we should hopefully see it built into the fabric of a civilization. We mentioned Egypt earlier. One of their problems from a geographical perspective was their lack of a fringe. The Nile River valley gave them great abundance, but immediately outside of that narrow strip of land lay the chaos of the desert.[23] They could conceive of the world only as a duality between chaos and order.

Greece, on the other hand, had a much different geography and a much different approach. The mountains and jagged coastline pushed most everyone within sight of the Mediterranean or Aegean Sea. We know that water often forms the boundary between different territories, be it a river, inlet, or ocean. Note then also how

---

22 Administrators, be careful of letting students discover this information, for herein lies a powerful argument in favor of untucked shirts.

23 The desert can be said to resemble the ocean in this respect. The desert has wave after wave of sand, with one dune indistinguishable from the next. We cannot live in the desert, though for the opposite reason of the ocean. In one, you die of too many things coming together, and in the other, of too many things going apart. But the result is the same.

many Greek stories and heroes involve water, such as *The Odyssey* and *Jason and the Argonauts*. Greek sculpture stressed fluid movement, in contrast to Egypt's emphasis on fixed positions.[24]

This level of comfort with the fluid fringe no doubt helped make ancient Greece a dynamic and creative civilization. Yet having such comfort with the fringe meant Greece experienced a great deal of division and ran through various political cycles quickly. Neil Young once sang that it was "better to burn out than to fade away," and if so, that description fits Greece.

Properly speaking, the fringe:

1. Serves as a mediator between order and chaos. We don't want only red and green lights on the road. Or, if you had to change your shower from hot to cold, you would want an in-between lukewarm as a buffer, or introduction, to what came next.

2. Functions as a protective layer for the core—think of the moat for a castle. Often, the people you need to do the "dirty work" for the core are not those who integrate easily into the core. Such fringe jobs help fringe people find their place in relation to the core.

Dogs in the ancient world tended to receive a lot of negative press. They resided outside the family core, the home/property. In ancient Rome, however, the "Lares"—dog-men—were revered as guardians of the property, depicted in many images with the heads of

---

24 Compare the following, for example: https://www.worldhistory.org/uploads/images/2174.jpg?v=1599314401, and https://www.christies.com/img/LotImages/2015/NYR/2015_NYR_03748_0045_000(a_greek_bronze_zeus_keraunios_hellenistic_period_circa_150-50_bc).jpg, with https://i.etsystatic.com/8729767/r/il/bfa3f0/1552888534/il_fullxfull.1552888534_m4au.jpg, and https://sculpture.solutions/wp-content/uploads/2021/02/egyptian-sculpture_4.jpg.

dogs and bodies of men,[25] matching the fluid nature of their border geography with their fluid physical form.[26]

Other images of lares have no direct dog theme, but Romans often depicted them with snakes, showing how the fringe can serve as a protection for the core (i.e., the home) against chaos.[27]

The fringe will always remain tricky. It can turn to chaos just as easily as it protects us from it. But it remains an integral part of the created order, and thus, of our classrooms. Teachers need to establish control of their environment, but we cannot have students genuflect before the order we create. Ultimately, our students leave our classrooms, with its attendant order, behind for hopefully bigger and better things. This order includes not just our class rules but also what and how we teach. For our classrooms to truly fractally reflect creation, we need a fringe to allow students to one day take their place at the head of the class.

Next we will examine the proper relationship between all three elements.

---

25   See, for example, this Roman denarius: https://i.pinimg.com/originals/f2/46/86/f246865bbf3f9d460b3bededaf29d738.jpg.

26   It makes sense to me that the ancient Egyptians revered cats. This reverence came from many reasons, no doubt, but cats often guard the interior—the core—from pests. Dogs have, until recently, been about the fringe. They hunt and explore far beyond the property lines. It seems no coincidence, then, that every American wilderness loner guy in movies has a dog. In addition, it seems obvious that Americans would revere dogs more than most any other culture. This fits with the fluidity of our civilization that has existed since its founding.

27   http://hablemosdemitologias.com/wp-content/uploads/2018/05/lares-2.jpg.

CHAPTER 8

Man as Macrocosm

So far, I hope we can see these elements of creation exist. For many of us, our intellectual training tells us these categories of thought may be nice illustrations of phenomena but are not really real. They might have convenience for us as a tool but have no direct authority over our interpretation of experience. They function as something like a linguistic convenience.

If these categories help you as mere conveniences, well and good. But I argue, in fact, that we encounter "real reality" with these categories. They have an existence that goes beyond analogy or metaphor.

For this to be true would mean finding the origin and anchor of this pattern in the life of God and, perhaps more specifically, in the reality of Christ Himself.

The Apostle John opens his gospel with, "In the beginning was the Word . . ." clearly meaning to reference Genesis 1. Many see John as viewing the Incarnation as a kind of second creation, and this has merit. I assert, however (along with others), that John tells us the Incarnation is *the* Creation event, from which everything radiates forward and backward. We should see Genesis 1, then, as an icon, or reflection of Christ Himself. The life of the Incarnate Christ, mysteriously slain before the foundation of the world (Rev. 13:8), forms the pattern of all things.

We see the interaction between the elements of core, fringe, and chaos in the life of Christ.

Christian tradition tells us that the angel Gabriel appears to Mary while she resides in the temple, weaving a curtain or veil. Thus, the Incarnation begins at the heart, the core, of the presence of God. Yet other elements of our tradition show us Gabriel appearing to Mary as she sat by a well. We should not see in this confusion about the exact historical details of the Annunciation. Rather, the Church reveals to us here a profound mystery.[28]

The temple represents solid space, water, fluid time.[29] In many ancient creation myths, and in Genesis 1, water represents chaos. Thus, right at the beginning of Christ's earthly existence, we see this interplay between core and chaos.

Christ's birth takes place at night, just as each day in Genesis 1 begins with evening. Mary gives birth in Bethlehem, a city on the fringe of Israelite society. The gospels of Luke and Matthew tell us that poor Jews and rich Gentiles come to see Christ in His infancy, giving us a chiasm of fringe people in the Jewish mindset.

---

28   If you go online and search for icons of the Annunciation, you will see examples of both, though most (I believe) will show Mary weaving in the Temple.

29   Churches that have holy water in their sanctuaries will place it right at the entrance to the nave. Thus, water forms the fluid boundary between holy spaces, between inner and outer courts, we might say.

Jesus and the Holy Family then travel to Egypt, in the desert, the land of sin and death. They travel from the fringe into chaos.

When we next encounter Christ, he is at the Temple, the core of God's presence.

We then see Christ with John the Baptist, certainly a fringe character. John wears clothes with a lot of fringes on them and eats unusual food. After His baptism, Christ moves to the wilderness, the realm of chaos, where He faces temptation. In his ministry, Christ associates with the fringe of Jewish society (the sinners and tax collectors) on the fringe of Jewish geography (i.e., Galilee) and does not return to Jerusalem—the core—until the end of His earthly life.

His death outside the city simultaneously brings together chaos and the new core of all things. Christ's sacrifice and descent into the earth conquers death. His resurrection and ascension to the right hand of the Father recreates the world, uniting the diversity and particularity of all things. Now, on this side of the resurrection, the "night and the day, are both alike" (cf. Ps. 139:12).

Many ancient philosophers and some early Christian writers talked of mankind as a microcosm of the cosmos. The universe obviously contains physical matter, and we are physical beings. But the ancients saw, too, that immaterial things existed, such as the soul, and ideas, and mankind has an immaterial aspect as well.

St. Maximus the Confessor, however, developed a more profound idea, that of man as macrocosm. For Christ transcends and governs all things, and all things cohere in Him (Col. 1:17). If we are "in Christ," as the Apostle wrote (cf. Rom. 5, Col. 2), then this truth should have profound implications for how we educate. Dumitru Stăniloae wrote in volume one of his *The Experience of God* that:

Some of the Fathers of the Church have said that man is a microcosm, a world which sums up in itself the larger world. Saint Maximus the Confessor remarked that the more correct way would be to consider man as a macrocosm because he is called to comprehend the whole world within himself, as one capable of comprehending it without losing himself, for he is distinct from the world. Therefore man effects a unity greater than the world exterior to himself whereas, on the contrary, the world as cosmos, as nature, cannot contain man fully within itself without losing him, that is, without losing in this way the most important reality, that part which more than all others gives reality its meaning. The idea that man is called to become "the world writ large" has a more precise expression, however, in the term macranthropos.

The term conveys the fact that in the strict sense the world is called to be humanized entirely, that is, to bear the entire stamp of the human, making real through that stamp a need that is implicit in the world's own meaning, to become in its entirety a humanized cosmos in a way that the human being is not called to become nor can ever fully become, even at the farthest limit of his attachment to the world where he is completely identified with it, a cosmosized man. The destiny of the cosmos is found in man, not man's destiny in the cosmos. This is shown, not only by the fact that the cosmos is the object of human consciousness and knowledge and not the reverse, but also by the fact that the entire cosmos serves human existence in a practical way.

Commenting on this remarkable insight, Macrina Walker writes:

Because of the position of the human in the cosmos, ultimately because the human is created in the image of God, the human person is a bond of the cosmos, or, looked at another way, the human person is priest of the cosmos. It is through the human that the cosmos relates to God. And it is in the human that the cosmos finds its meaning. But, conversely, if the human person fails to fulfill such a priestly, interpretative, relating role, then that failure is not just a personal, individual failing, it is a failing with cosmic consequences.

We are becoming dimly aware of this as we realize how human behavior that fails to recognize the integrity of God's creation, its inherent value, its inherent beauty, and treats it simply as so much material to be consumed, how such behavior is more than simply self-destructive, or destructive of human society, but threatens the ordered beauty of the cosmos itself.

According to St. Maximus, man as microcosm places him in a "middle position" on earth, or rather between heaven and earth, and gives him a specific task: that of mediation. By mediating between and connecting oppositions in himself as microcosm, the same thing is achieved in the macrocosm.[30]

In the coming chapters, I will seek to unpack just a few implications of what this means for how we teach, but before we get to applying this reality, we have another pattern to uncover, that of uniting heaven and earth.

---

30   https://avowofconversation.wordpress.com/2009/04/30/the-human-person-as-priest-of-the-cosmos/.

CHAPTER 9

Rocky Soil

*B**ehold, a sower went out to sow . . . Some seed fell on stony places, where they did not have much earth; and they immediately sprang up because they had no depth of earth. But when the sun was up they were scorched, and because they had no root they withered away (Mt. 13:3,6)."*

No doubt you have had the following experience, likely many times . . .

You attend an educational conference and listen to a speaker plant an idea, a seed of sorts, into your mind. Let us suppose you hear, "Teachers need to teach children with a full understanding that they are made in the image of God." This makes you reflect on your own educational experience, and you realize you were treated more like a cog in a giant machine or "another brick in the wall." This phrase struck other faculty members as well, and you plan to talk through it at teacher training several weeks hence. You get excited about that prospect because your brain is firing off in so many directions. Where might this lead?

By the time you discuss the concept with your colleagues, however, something seems lost. You collectively still appreciate the power of the speaker's words. But when you get together, everyone has their own take, and you find the idea has potentially a million different applications. We all know that if it has that many possibilities, it might as well have none at all.

Or suppose someone shares the idea that teachers should show more patience in the classroom. This idea also strikes a chord inside you. You remember a time when, yes, you should have had more grace with student X that one time. You remember the patience and long-suffering of God. But then this idea dies on the vine as well. After all, previous to hearing this, it wasn't as if you had a strong commitment to being *impatient* with your students.

But even if you determine that you should show more patience, you quickly realize, *More patience . . . relative to what, exactly?* If every student except a few perfectly understood the formulas, would you "show patience" and not move to the next lesson? If so, for how long would you show patience? Maybe a particular student needs more time to figure something out on their own, and you should give them that time Or, you surmise, maybe he's going about it all the wrong way and needs some intervention from you to get on the right track. Or maybe you just move on. Which is the best course, and what has this to do with the idea, the seed, about patience in the first place?

In the section cited in the parable of the sower, the seed is good, but we lack the proper "earth" for the seed to take root. We have "heaven" in the form of the idea but not enough proper context and no means to unite the two if we could.

In previous chapters, we examined the pattern of core, chaos, and the fringe that lies between them. One might roughly call this pattern the "side-to-side" pattern, which involves navigating horizontal space. Our next pattern involves how to go "up and down," how to navigate the union of heaven and earth.

CHAPTER 10

The Mountain

Mankind has always attributed a sacrality to mountains. One easily thinks of Mt. Olympus and the seven hills of Rome. Many Buddhists consider Mt. Everest a holy place, and also Mt. Kallash. Many interesting theories surround Egypt's pyramids, with one possible explanation being that they had no natural mountains near them, so they built some.[31]

Mountains play a significant role in redemptive history. Eden resided on a mountain (Ez. 28). We recall Mt. Sinai, Mt. Carmel, Mt. Nebo, Mt. Zion, the Sermon on the Mount, and Golgotha itself, the "hill of the skull." The list could continue. We must conclude that the universality of the importance of mountains constitutes something much more than a pagan distortion. Given the religious testimony of the ages, we can say that one goes to a mountain when one wants to meet God.

---

31   This might partly explain why the pyramid-building era in Egypt may have lasted, according to some, only a bit more than a century, but I offer this theory very hesitantly.

We could suggest many reasons for the role mountains have in civilization. They serve as images of stability and grandeur. They inspire awe. More importantly, however, they show us a union of heaven and earth, something we cannot just see but experience. If we climb mountains, the summit gives us an uncanny, all-encompassing view of our surroundings. We see the spatial relationships between everything that surrounds us. However, at the summit, one loses focus on the particulars below that we can see with much greater clarity at the mountain's base.[32]

This ascending-descending-ascending pattern reveals itself throughout Scripture. Adam and Eve lose communion with God and must descend the mountain. In Jacob's dream in Genesis 29, he sees angels ascending and descending a ladder, with God pronouncing His blessing over Jacob.[33] This dream reflects creation itself, as from chaos (sleep, which is a mini death) comes "creation," that is the Incarnation and Christ's reconciliation of heaven and earth.

Space will not permit me to examine every case of the mountain imagery in Scripture, but Mt. Sinai may be the most emblematic. Here Moses goes up the mountain to receive the light and the seed of the law of God. But as he ascends, a rift between heaven and earth

---

32 From reading a variety of mountain-climbing disaster books, one common theme emerges: climbers mentally and physically forget about the descent. The summit entrances them, in a sense, and they forget that for their mountaintop experience to truly be integrated into their lives, they have to climb back down successfully.

33 Much more could be said about this remarkable story. First, we see that Jacob rests his head (the "heavenly" part of ourselves) upon a stone, from the earth, giving us a picture in miniature of the union of heaven and earth lost at the Fall. Second, we see that after this in Gen. 29, Jacob meets Rachel. This marriage (marriage is itself a picture of the union of heaven and earth [cf. Eph. 5]), is frustrated, however, by Laban. The full union of heaven and earth has yet to come. Third, some early iconographic depictions of Jacob's ladder include an image of Jacob embracing the Angel of the Lord after wrestling with Him, showing the dream as a foretaste of a reunion of heaven and earth.

occurs, for at the bottom of the mountain we see chaos, idol worship, and the triumph of the Devil (Ex. 32).[34]

Mt. Sinai has its partner in Mt. Tabor, traditionally viewed as the site of the Transfiguration (Mt. 17, Lk. 9).[35] Here, Jesus ascends and reveals Himself bathed in light. But just as the people could not bear the light that shone from Moses, so, too, the light from Christ blinds and confuses Peter, James, and John. They cannot see or perceive clearly. At the bottom of Mt. Tabor, the other disciples abide in confusion and chaos as demons hold sway over the multitude. Jesus in turn tells them that they lack the true seed of faith. They were not sufficiently heavenly minded (Mt. 17:20–21, Mk. 9:29).[36]

The descent of Christ, beginning with the Incarnation, continues after His death.[37] He continues down into the very realm of death and hell, but from that point, the worm turns, as they say. His Resurrection and Ascension completes His victory. Now our elder brother (Rom. 8:29) sits as Man, in the Holy of Holies. Human flesh resides without shame or blemish in the presence of God. After the Ascension, the Spirit of God descends at Pentecost.

---

34   Ex. 24:9–18 tells us that Aaron and the elders went halfway up the mountain with Moses, with Moses and Joshua to continue farther up. Aaron and the others came down the mountain, and when this happened, the people's link between heaven and earth disappeared, with the golden calf as the result.

35   Some recently have suggested Mt. Hermon for the location. Origin, and St. Cyril of Jerusalem, among others, believe it to have been Mt. Tabor.

36   Here we see a link between prayer—focusing on heaven—and fasting, which makes us "lighter" and able ascend the mountain of God more easily.

37   We see the paradoxical nature of Christ's death in that (1) the death of the Son of God was the world's greatest evil, bringing Him into the very bowels of the earth, and (2) we exalt the cross for all to see. We hold it high, for Christ's death and "descent" took place at the top of a "mountain" (the Hill of the Skull). The crucifixion lives out Christ's words to ascend by going down (Eph. 4:10, Lk. 14:10).

At Pentecost, all hear the same message, but in their own tongue (Acts 2). God gives unity without eroding particularity, uniting heaven and earth (i.e., the summit and base of the mountain).[38]

As we should expect, this principle of the union of heaven and earth extends from Christ and Scripture to all of life. The very act of perception itself witnesses to this.[39] No necessary reason exists that we should perceive coherent objects. Yet we see things like bowls, bottles, chairs, and countless other things every day. We could in theory reside at the "bottom of the mountain" and declare that the distinctions we make between things have no basis in reality. "It is arbitrary," some might say, "to declare this particular group of atoms a chair, when those so-called 'chair atoms' are just like any other atoms." Here we have the problem of too much diversity.

But this "diversity" problem has its mirror image in caring only about the top of the mountain. From the summit, we can easily lose sight of proper distinctions between things and blend too much together. Whether we give too much unity to our experience, or too much diversity, we get the same result. We cannot make proper distinctions between things and cannot interact with the world we inhabit. For we need not doubt that to exist, we must see distinct things such as water and cups from which to drink that water. We must distinguish between green beans and the green grass, though both are plants that arise from the earth.[40]

---

38   Pentecost reflects the same unity and diversity of Christ Himself, fully God and fully man, one person with two natures, as the Council of Chalcedon (AD 451) admirably defines and confesses.

39   I am very much indebted to Jonathan Pageau primarily, and Jordan Peterson secondarily, for this insight.

40   This failure to perceive rightly from either not enough unity or not enough particularity mirrors the chaos and death brought about by either the desert or the flood, as discussed earlier.

With the side-to-side pattern of core, fringe, and chaos, and the up-and-down pattern of the mountain and the union of heaven and earth now established, we can move on later to applying this pattern in the cosmos of our classrooms.

CHAPTER 11

"The Sabbath was made for Man"

Token his image of a mountain has significance in so far as it shows us an image of stability, unity, and diversity. More importantly, we see Christ enact and embody the pattern of the mountain. But we should not think of Christ conforming to a pattern so much as the pattern reflecting Him.

In turn, we should not think about the world anthropomorphically, but theo-morphically, or perhaps "Christo-morphically."

We should see the world, then, as made by Christ and through Him. Yes, Christ is the new Adam, but in some ways, Adam was made in the image of Christ, "slain before the foundation of the world" (Rev. 13:8).[41] Thus, we can see mountain imagery reflecting all of humanity as well as Christ, for He is our elder brother (Heb. 2:11–12). The mountain reflects the Man and all men.[42]

We see this in the structure of the human body. The top of the mountain reflects our heads, the "heavenly" part of us, our intellect.

Our thoughts form the seed, if you will, of our actions. Through our intellect, we can comprehend the whole in a moment of thought. And yet we cannot live in our heads. Thought must come down into action.

Most every other creature walks with all their legs on the ground, showing their "earthly" orientation. We have just two of our appendages on the ground, with our heads erect, showing our heavenly and earthly natures, just as Christ is God and man, heaven and earth.

When we put things into the earth, they break down. This fragmentation and loss of form brings a kind of chaos and death from which new life arises. The seed, which comes from above, must be buried and die (John 12:24). The earth reflects our bellies, our lower parts. Why pray and give thanks before meals? One can think of many reasons, but primarily, we should understand eating as a type of death and resurrection miracle. We put dead things into our "earth," and new life (of a kind) arises from our stomach, which breaks down our food just as the earth decomposes organic matter.

Our appetites, our emotions, all serve a purpose and have God as their author. But they abide in us often without form. As C. S. Lewis noted in his wonderful essay "Men Without Chests," our heart mediates between our intellect and our emotions. Our heart unites heaven and earth, containing not some of each but all of both.

---

41   As a quick example of this, some early church fathers (Tertullian, Methodius of Phillipi, and especially St. Hilary of Poitier) sees the creation of Eve through the sleep of Adam as a type of the birth of the Church through the death of Christ and Adam awakening as a type of the resurrection. St. Hilary writes in his *Tractatus Mysteriorum*, "We must see in Adam's sleep and Eve's formation the revelation of a hidden mystery concerning Christ and the Church. . . . That is why the Heavenly Adam, after the sleep of his Passion, recognized in the Church His own bone and flesh . . ." Cited in Jean Daniélou's illuminating *From Shadows to Reality: Studies in the Biblical Typology of the Fathers*, Chapter IV.

42   Again, I must credit Jonathan Pageau, who has much to say on the topic here (and other places): https://www.youtube.com/watch?v=RupeqP3GS6k.

Seeing the world and oneself in this manner may be new to some readers and hopefully interesting and illuminating for all. But like all truth, it has a practical point. In life, politics, and in education, people often ask us to contemplate abstractions or random points of data, to look at the clouds or bits of grass and rock. When we attempt to cram our students into a "curriculum," we lose sight of our feet on the ground. When we focus merely on the needs and wants of particular students, we forget that we have to *ascend together*. To get *the* mountain, we need the whole man, body and soul.

PART II

Applying the Patterns

CHAPTER 12

Forming the Core, Part 1

Okay, so all of this has been enormously fascinating, no doubt. But I jibed at speakers who only give big ideas that have no way to land, and so I hope not to repeat that mistake. I alluded to the enormous number of decisions teachers must make and how this can sap the energy and confidence of teachers. Schools, in turn, want to avoid teacher burnout so their teachers can push past the first few critical years. Confident, experienced teachers make fewer mistakes and allow schools to start building a robust faculty culture. With a healthy faculty culture in place, a healthy school culture follows.

We'll begin at the beginning, with a teacher forming the core of their classroom.

When I first started teaching at Ad Fontes, we had only three full-time staff, and one of them was Mrs. A. I had never taught in a classroom before and knew I had to learn fast. I watched Mrs. A to try and pick up some pointers. She had a wonderful teaching style. She controlled the class mostly through her manner and personality. She glided calmly back and forth, exuding grace and gentility in the best aristocratic tradition. Gruff and coarse guys fell under her spell, and, of course, the young ladies all aspired to be Mrs. A.

I at least had the brains to notice this worked, so I tried it myself. After about a week of failing entirely, I needed a new plan. I could in no way exude the soft-spoken charm of Mrs. A. I flailed around for a while and eventually discovered I taught better as myself rather than someone else. Though it took about twelve to eighteen months to leverage my own personality in the classroom, I had stumbled on an important truth: if man truly is a macrocosm, the teacher, not the rules and not the curriculum, must serve as the core of their cosmos/ classroom. Just as man mediates creation back to God, the teacher serves as the point of mediation between the student and that which they need to learn (what resides at the mountaintop). Teach, then, through your personality. I have had one minor role in exactly one play, and from that extensive experience, I can say that pretending to be someone else, while fun, also drains you quickly.[43]

How this happens depends on the individual, of course, but I have seen a variety of approaches work well over the years:

- One teacher had a military background and so at times he strode more pointedly, spoke more loudly and definitively, than any other teacher. Almost always, the students ate it up.

- One young female teacher (Miss B) enjoyed wearing dress scarves with her outfits on occasion. She

____

43   I once heard actor Gabriel Byrne (*Miller's Crossing, The Usual Suspects*, etc.) argue against the so-called method school that encourages an actor to in essence *become* the character one is playing. Byrne thought one should always play oneself but you play yourself happy, sad, etc. as the script requires. I think this insight can apply to teaching, where one plays perhaps a slightly tweaked version of oneself in the classroom.

never drew attention to them herself, but eventually her female students noticed (the guys wouldn't have known what they themselves wore on any given day, let alone anyone else). In time, a large handful of younger ladies in her class would seek to wear scarves like their teacher when they could.

- A young male elementary teacher (Mr. C) took to wearing bow ties frequently. He had an impressive collection. Not every guy can pull off bow ties, which require a certain panache. This teacher had it, and so eventually he had many of his students voluntarily wearing ties on "Bow Tie Tuesdays."

If you execute this well, you will generate attention, and this attention will turn into a kind of power.

Some may read the above paragraphs and surmise that I want cult leaders for teachers. I don't mind going on the record for this one—cult leaders are bad. Don't be one![44] Your job as a teacher means to take the attention you generate and pass it on to what you point to. For the literature teacher, it means pointing to Homer, the math teacher to Euclid, and so on.

Most every guy never wore a bow tie again after they left Mr. C's class. When the young ladies of Miss B's class got a bit older and made their own fashion decisions, very few wore a neck scarf. That never bothered either one of them. If you envision it bothering you, please avoid the teaching profession.

---

44   Cult leaders often have bad ends because no one is meant to be the focal point of too much attention for too long. It destroys a person, warping their perception of reality. When one can no longer perceive reality rightly, the end can't be far away. Teachers who fall into this trap may be the darling of many students for a time, but the fall will come, and it will be hard and definitive.

CHAPTER 13

Forming the Core, Part 2

Like any nation, America has its strengths and weaknesses. Some of these strengths come from good fortune. For example, the cushion of two oceans helped protect us from the horrors of twentieth-century warfare. But Dame Fortune has a flip side that also adds to our weaknesses, such as the fact that we have very little history as a nation. Most other cultures have their foundations in a mythic or quasi-mythic past. As such, their founding cannot come under critical examination. Hence, Egyptians, the Chinese, the French—they simply accept this crucial part of national belonging. But America's founding happened quite recently, and this allows for everyone to have a look and have their say. We have no unquestioned origin story, and this contributes to our current identity crisis as a nation and will continue to do so in the future. When something comes up for debate, it comes up for analysis, and ultimately, deconstruction. This cannot happen to the core.

Some things in life have variability to them, and some things just are. The buck must stop somewhere. Some atheists and agnostics, for example, complain that God has no one to answer to. Of course, whatever or whomever God answered to would be God, or, failing that, matter and mechanical processes are "God." The buck must stop somewhere.

In your classroom, offer no explanation or defense for what you want to comprise the core of your cosmos. If you want a seating chart, just tell the students where they sit. Students may not like the seating chart and may question why. If you say, "So you won't talk to each other during class," you've lost the game. They will respond with, "But we won't talk. Give us a chance!" and now you are on your heels. The seating chart will bring contention the rest of the year. You will likely end up abandoning it.

When it comes to the core, Yoda's dictum rings true: "Do or do not. There is no try."

Very young students will accept an unlimited amount of almost anything. As students get older, they naturally accept much less, and the teacher needs more careful thought about the composition of the core. A class with juniors and seniors should have a smaller core and larger fringe than one with eighth graders. But the principle remains: whatever forms the core simply "is."

Since the core deals with the "it just is" of things, recall mythology and pay close attention to origins. I remember my daughter talking to me once about a particular teacher. She admitted that this teacher sometimes had class management issues but had one very consistent strength: students always knew when class began. He used the same phrases, the same prayer, every day, every class. It worked.

Adopt an unquestioned method of opening class as a way of forming an unquestioned origin to your cosmos.[45]

Of course, how you begin the year with your students in those first few days will go a long way toward forming the core. Plan them well. Some teachers load up too much on rules, procedures, and the like. Such things have their place, but spend no more than five minutes on this, especially for older students. You, the teacher, form the central part of the core, not the rules. You, and not the rules, control the class. But going the boring and pedantic route toward core formation is infinitely preferable to getting creative with the core.[46] This creativity comes in two deadly forms, both related to each other.

The first comes in the form of the "relatable" teacher. Here, the teacher starts the year nice and easy—"Let's not make things too burdensome. Let's get to know one another," and so on. A friend of mine related that he tried this his first year of teaching many years ago. "Hey guys, I'm Mr. Rockstar, your teacher. I enjoy hiking. I like the Counting Crows and Birkenstocks. You know . . . I just happened to bring my guitar. Maybe we could sing a song or two."

I exaggerated what he said a bit, but you get the gist.

He mentioned that for about two weeks, he bathed in glory, hearing comments in the hall such as "Mr. Rockstar is cool, man,

---

45   In Christian schools, many teachers begin their class with prayer, and this is good. But some want to mix it up by asking for volunteers—"Who will pray today?" and so on. When this happens, there is a pause. People look around. Eventually, someone raises their hand reluctantly. Or maybe a few people raise their hands. Now you have an extra decision to make. Who will you pick? And who did you pick yesterday? At the core, keep it simple. Have a set way to begin your class.

46   Of course, there is nothing wrong with creativity. But creativity means fluidity, and you don't want any water eroding your foundation.

much better than Mrs. X from last year." "For sure, man, English is my favorite class."

Who said teaching was hard?

Then, inevitably, familiarity bred contempt. The backlash came fast and furious. He lost all control of his students, and it took him months to regain it.

The next year, he corrected this mistake with a different opening speech. "Hello, my name is Mr. Wright. Welcome to English 9. In this class, we diagram sentences. Open the books already on your desk to page three, where we begin with number one . . ."

Perhaps an overcorrection, but still vastly preferable to "Relatable Guy." His students listened to him and learned English. He had no problems with behavior issues that year. Teachers who go for "relatable" forget their students already have friends. Hopefully, you, the teacher, have them as well. That helps avoid the "Relatable Guy" mistake.[47]

The second error is a rarer, deadlier form of the same basic disease, known as TTBRWIDPSS (Trying to be Robin Williams in *Dead Poets Society* Syndrome).[48] Here, the teacher starts the year by trying to subvert the very concept of the core itself. On the first day of class, you take the students outside, you ask them to look at the sky and the flowers, to write how chemistry makes them feel, and reminisce about the time you got a crocodile in spelling.[49] Only one teacher in a thousand could pull off this kind of high-wire act. Chances are you are not that guy, and Robin Williams was an actor in a fictional story.

---

47   If you can pull it off naturally, being confused and out of touch, à la "Unfrozen Caveman Lawyer" (https://www.youtube.com/watch?v=500oUCdpdgU), can work well.

48   I really do not like this movie.

49   Shout out to *Arrested Development*, Season 1, Episode 10.

A weird thought . . . if it is the first day of biology class, maybe teach some biology.

Every teenager ranks "sense of humor" very high on their list of qualities they desire for their future spouse. Adults know that, yes, a sense of humor can serve as a great asset in a relationship, but it can never be its foundation. By their nature, cores are humdrum and ordinary, but such is the stuff of life. Part of the teacher's task involves showing students the beauty of the ordinary.

But sometimes even the best-laid plans . . .

I have taught ancient history to eighth graders for about twenty years. To this day, it remains one of my favorite classes, and I feel I have command over the material. After a few years of fiddling, I arrived at an opening day routine that always seemed to work. Except for one year when it didn't. After my opening five minutes, I usually see a few quizzical glances and furrowed brows. I know I've set the hook. On this occasion, I got nothing at all except dead eyes and blank faces. I moved on to my standard opening questions, which usually put four or five hands in the air. This time, crickets. Their arms remained firmly at their sides.

I fidgeted with my hands a bit. The confident tones in my voice dissipated. I spoke more haltingly. Time slowed to a crawl. I looked at the clock. Surely class was almost over? Alas, no—thirty-eight minutes left!

When the core seems to turn against you, when chaos barges through the gates, what can you do?[50] How can you set things to rights? We will examine this in the next chapter.

---

50   Some may balk at my use of the term "chaos" for this situation. Surely there are worse things than a group of students sitting quietly. All one could say here is the students were not really caring, and that is normal. When I was a student, I cared not all about a great many things. I use "chaos" in the sense that Jordan Peterson defines the term in chapter 2 of his *Maps of Meaning*. For Peterson, chaos is a place or psychological state where one does not know how to act, where normal expectations of how we interact with one another disappear. In this case, the students may not have felt the presence of chaos, but I sure did!

CHAPTER 14

Taming Chaos

We live in confusing times, and our inability to understand the role of the "other" contributes a great deal to our predicament.[51] On the one hand, elements of the political left have those who not only want to experience the "other"—whether that be unfamiliar places, experiences, people, cultures, or ideas—but in fact seek to idolize it. For this group, other cultures always have something to teach the West, while the West consistently harms the rest of the world. And yet some of these same people also demand "safe spaces," where "walls" will protect them from ideas or experiences they wish to avoid.

In turn, some on the political right have tightened in unusual ways. We see the rise of political populism everywhere in the Western

---

51   The early portions of this chapter once again owe a great debt to Jonathan Pageau's thoughts on chaos. A few examples of his comments on this topic can be found here: https://www.youtube.com/watch?v=OcvUK80ROGs and https://www.youtube.com/watch?v=u7BQaQE_Jn8.

world. Such parties usually advocate for tighter borders and tighter restrictions on trade and the movement of labor. And yet some elements on the political right also put a large emphasis on individual freedoms and the freedom of the market to provide almost any good or service to anyone. Certainly, both sides of our political spectrum have their internal incongruities, and this makes dialogue between them very difficult.[52]

In truth, the "other" is neither bad nor good in itself. The moral impact of the other depends largely on context. What will always be true, however, is that the other will destabilize existing situations, and this, too, brings good or bad depending on the context. The other, then, functions as a kind of chaos.

Wisdom means knowing how to use chaos for good when it comes, if possible. Our instincts tell us to lash out against it, but this will rarely work. Recall my example in the last chapter about the "chaotic" situation I faced. Imagine me getting upset, saying something like, "Hey everyone, wake up! This is good material! Other students showed a lot more interest than you, so get with the program!" We all know I would have dug myself a deeper hole. At that point in the class, I had ceased to act as the focal point of their attention. Regaining attention effectively takes more than a mere use of force.

Sometimes as parents we pretend not to see certain things our kids do, and sometimes this is for the best. Sometimes we lack the energy to engage profitably, and sometimes we should let them work

---

52   Science fiction can be a great venue for understanding this open/closed dynamic. Think of a movie like *The Shape of Water*, where the "monster" gets mistreated by our society and the heroine not only protects the monster but falls in love with him. The *Alien* movie series takes the opposite approach. In *Aliens*, for example, Paul Reiser's character (Carter Burke) wants to study and learn from the deadly creatures, and he is smarmy, cowardly, and devious. *Close Encounters of the Third Kind* and *Independence Day* reflect these dual dynamics in different ways.

things out themselves. Tomorrow is another day, after all. So, too, teachers in my described situation might just put their heads down and plow ahead. "I'll get 'em next time," we say to ourselves. This strategy has merit, and certainly I've used it many times. Retreat and trade space for time.

But another possibility exists, one that we teachers rarely consider.

The world is round, no doubt for many reasons, and surely the fact of its circular nature teaches us something. We know that when you have traveled a certain distance, the fastest way back to where you began means not pulling back but pushing forward. So, too, when a person, a situation, or an argument pushes against you, sometimes you harden its position by pushing against it. Perform a jujitsu move, on the other hand, and you regain control. Chaos accumulates power through the attempted imposition of a weak form of order. In that eighth-grade class, on that day, I occupied a weak position.

So I stopped talking and paused for a slightly awkward length of time. Some of them noticed the silence. Some continued their glassy stare, no doubt content in their happy places.

I then asked, "Did any of your moms get the Aquafresh toothpaste on sale at Costco this week?"[53]

Costco sells in bulk. One cannot just buy *a* tube of toothpaste. Earlier that week, Costco had started their new monthly sales, and one could obtain eight tubes of Aquafresh Extreme Clean for something like eight dollars. We bought it ourselves. But this particular Aquafresh variety went all out. I'm guessing they badly wanted you to believe that their toothpaste *really, truly* worked. I suppose that, along with enamel and gum lining, it also removed plaque. Using

---

53 No sense in asking if your "parents" got the toothpaste. We all know that no male can find anything at any time in that store.

that toothpaste set my mouth aflame, and we had eight tubes of the stuff left to go.

I could reasonably guess that a variety of my students' parents went to Costco. And that Aquafresh coupon got pole position in the monthly coupon book, as it's the kind of product almost every household needs.

A few hands went up. I had their attention now, but the hands were raised tentatively.

I took another step. "Did it, like"—I had to say "like," of course—"set your mouth on fire?"

Please, please, please, please, please, please.

"Yes!" Billy blurted out. "I said, 'Mom, this toothpaste burns my mouth!' And she was like, 'I don't care. Use it anyway.' And I was like, 'No way, Mom. I can't do that!'"

Jenny and Joey joined in with similar comments, and the floodgates burst. Everyone suddenly absolutely needed to tell everyone else about the toothpaste they liked and didn't like.

Now, in some ways, I still had chaos. But the worm had turned, for now they were at least talking about something I had introduced. After a few minutes of this, someone asked, "Mr. Mathwin, what does this have to do with history class?"

I thought for a moment. "Nothing at all. But it was on my mind. And, speaking of things on my mind, history, don't you know, can be an interesting field of study."

They groaned, but . . . they were groaning, not staring blankly. They, in fact, had the right reaction for the situation.

Order restored. The rest of class went much like those in previous years.

You can turn a negative number positive, but you can't just throw positive integers at -458. You need to double down and multiply it with another negative number. When that happens, presto, you turn things right side up once again.

Chaos always destabilizes. When you put something into the earth, darkness surrounds it, and soon it begins to break apart and die. But this chaos also creates an opportunity for something new, and perhaps even something better, to emerge. For the rest of the year, students remembered when "Mr. Mathwin talked about toothpaste in class," and this cachet carried me a long way with that group.

This is the "trick" inherent in nature when you bury a seed. It is the trick Christ pulled on the Devil with His own death. If we keep our heads and get a bit lucky, teachers can use chaos against itself in a similar way to give our classrooms new life.[54]

In this way, chaos as the unfamiliar other comes to destroy you, but it also offers an opportunity.

54   J. R. R. Tolkien was steeped in traditional languages and literature, so he understood this traditional pattern involving chaos very well. We note how Bilbo used the dragon's vanity against himself to reveal his weak spot, and how in *Farmer Giles of Ham*, the main character used guile to tame the crafty dragon. In *The Lord of the Rings*, the good guys defeat Sauron not through direct force but by using direct force as a smokescreen for the bait and switch at Mt. Doom.

CHAPTER 15

Chaos and the Body

One of the key principles of this book is that the structure of the world we encounter is not arbitrary but a clue to meaning. This applies not just to creation in a general way but to the human body specifically.

Most of the time, we have control over our bodies. We decide to speak, to move, to eat, and so forth. But at times, chaos washes over us and we lose control. Take crying, for example. Most of us have little to no control over this. We start weeping and sometimes cannot make ourselves stop. The same holds for laughter. We likely have all had the experience of being doubled over laughing or falling out of our chair.[55] Sleep gives us another pertinent example. We

---

55 We should note that tears and laughter are close allies. Both deconstruct the order of our bodies, just as they deconstruct the order in a particular social setting. We usually feel better after experiencing both. Tears can turn into laughter, and laughter produces tears. This is another living example of the round nature of the world. That is, when opposites keep going in their respective directions, they eventually meet.

can provide conditions for sleep, but we cannot make ourselves sleep. Sleep comes to us unbidden.

Teachers often get unnerved when a student falls asleep, and this makes sense when we remember that sleep is a form of chaos in your classroom. But teachers need to exercise caution in how they react. If sleep is chaos, we must first realize that the student probably had no intention of falling asleep or even intended disrespect.[56] Alas, often those who want to actively undermine your world are wide awake.

But neither can one ignore the chaos in the room.[57]

Teachers have many good reasons for showing a video during a particular class. For one, pressing play is an easy lesson plan, and sometimes teachers need a break. Of course, the same holds for students. Hopefully by now, the reader has an inkling that showing videos signals that one has reached a fringe of sorts and teachers and students have permission to relax. If at all possible, don't schedule such relaxation events unless one has reached the proper point in the cycle of time for a particular week.

So about once a month for "Fun Fridays," I show a video. Students generally get excited for videos because it means no note-taking, no one will ask them questions, and so on. Invariably, they will ask to turn off the lights and draw the blinds when watching. I usually like to go along with such simple requests. In addition, the lack of light can give a slightly more dramatic atmosphere to seeing a wispy-haired man with a British accent discuss the "papacy" (with the first *a*

---

56   I remember fighting sleep almost all the time in one of my favorite professor's classes in grad school. It had nothing to do with the teacher and everything to do with the time of day, as the class met 3:00–5:00 p.m.

57   My father taught for more than thirty-five years and once remarked to me that one of his great regrets was humiliating a student who had fallen asleep. Handle the sleeping student gently—maybe they don't feel well, maybe they had to stay up late, etc. Occasionally it can be used for humor, but the sleeping student cannot be the butt of the joke. However you choose to handle sleep, students need to know you are not fazed by chaos.

pronounced not as in "paper" but as in "pad"). Sometimes you need all the help you can get.

But if you allow darkness, you risk courting chaos. Just this past year with my eighth-grade class, some students had a hard time staying awake during videos.[58] This happened in the second semester, when we met for class second-to-last period, a time of day and week (this was on Fridays, remember) when students already have a foot out the door. Showing videos made sense during a natural loosening moment, but sleeping in class, even during a video, presents a problem. The problem involved me as well—I also sometimes fell asleep!

A teacher has two options here. Our instinct for establishing order likely would push us to the following:

1. Turn the lights back on, walk around the room, make sure no one sleeps.

2. Have students take notes during the video and turn them in after class, or quiz them on the video, with a particular focus on the sections where a student or two slept.

These options, however, send a schizophrenic message about time to your students. On the one hand, you say, "We can relax," by showing a movie, and on the other, "but not too much!" Imagine a parent saying, "Let's go get ice cream!" and then adding, "When we get home, I'll quiz you on the store's thirty-one flavors."[59] We need to avoid such mixed messages.

---

58   This story actually happened as I relate it.

59   Teachers should be honest with themselves about what kind of video they show. Some videos have really good, insightful stuff in them, and some we show aren't very good but we do it to fill time. You can sometimes ask students to take notes on the former. I would never recommend this for the latter, especially as a punishment. If you yourself don't really believe in what you do, students will quickly pick up on that and act accordingly. Tighten up only when and where you really have to.

Another possibility presents itself. Even a great video will not have much penetration with eighth graders on Friday afternoon. If not a lot of curricular learning will take place regardless of what you do, focus on accomplishing something adjacent to the curriculum by using the advantages of the fringe.[60]

I decided to institute the following measures:

1. We should all try not to fall asleep, but I will keep the lights off (challenge accepted!).

2. If you fall asleep, we will of course wake you, and for the next "Fun Friday" video, you have to bring in cookies, doughnuts, etc. for the class.

Immediately, as one would expect, the question arose: "What happens if you fall asleep, Mr. Mathwin?" Obviously, I bound myself to the same code and, in fact, had to provide treats twice during the remainder of the year. What can I say? I'm getting old.

Having taken account of the presence of chaos, my students now knew how to act within it. Students need not feel alarmed if someone slept during a video. The plan had a two-fold effect. First, students tried harder to stay awake. Second, it allowed for the student (or . . . teacher) who fell asleep to redeem themselves. Sleeping cast them outside the community, so to speak. A student (or . . . teacher) could be lightly teased for falling outside the established norms. But once the offender provided the appropriate gifts, all order got restored and all light poking fun ceased. Classroom expectations and social dynamics, your "cosmos," have recreated themselves.

---

60   You will only feel like you are cheating students in this case if you think the curriculum, or the facts of history, etc., are the main point of the class. Adjusting in this case does not mean the students are running the asylum but that you are tacking together with proper pattern recognition.

We can also take the example of laughter.[61] A few years ago, I walked into a different eighth-grade class on a Wednesday morning.[62] Usually I used Wednesdays for hard work, but I wanted to change it up. "Clear your desks, everyone. No notes today. We're doing something different!"

One of the more exuberant students, John, stood up at his desk, said, "Yes!" and with a wide sweeping motion of his hand, pushed his notebook off his table, where it clattered on the floor, scattering his pens and pencils. A few started laughing and immediately looked to me for my reaction. What would I do?

Before we get to that, another story involving junior high students laughing . . .

Many years before the above story happened, very early in my career, I taught a Bible class to a combined group of seventh and eighth graders. The class had spirit, and I lacked the skills to manage them well. The topic of the deity of Christ came up, and we discussed it. Some good questions led a bit deeper into the weeds. I decided to bring up the Nicene Creed and the term *homoousias*, meaning the "same nature,"[63] (i.e., Christ the Son is of the same nature as the Father).

---

61   I recall a comment of Mel Brooks to Jerry Seinfeld, in a *Comedians in Cars Getting Coffee* episode. Jerry asked about the origin of Brooks's famous play *The Producers*, which Jerry saw as a way for Brooks to get revenge of sorts on Hitler. Brooks mentioned that "You can't out-tirade Hitler! You have to find another way." In this case, laughter was Brooks's "other way." Nothing deconstructs a malign order quite as well as laughter. To prevent laughter from destroying the order you construct, make it a part of the order itself, like a medieval king having his fool at court.

62   I realize most of my stories involve eighth graders. This was not my intention when beginning the book, but it is good evidence for why that age is so fun to teach.

63   At the council, the heretic Arius and his supporters argued for *homoiousious*, which would have meant Christ had a similar nature as the Father but not the same nature.

I remember quite distinctly writing the word on the board, my back to the class, looking at it for a second, realizing immediately (but still too late), *I've made a huge mistake.*[64]

Sure enough, Doug piped up and asked, "Are you saying God is a homo?" Some laughter and some wide-eyed looks followed. Doug was a good kid but one who often let his mouth get him into trouble. I absolutely should have sent him to the office. Instead, I said something lame like, "That's disrespectful," and tried to move on. But you can't move on from that! With my weak sauce response, and obvious fear in the face of chaos, the students lost confidence in me. Alas, with something so obviously out of bounds, no histrionics would have been required. A simple "Those comments are unacceptable, and you must go to the office" would have sufficed.

I can attribute my failure to throw him out to rookie jitters. A new teacher sending someone to the office is akin to diving into the deep end for the first time. It usually requires a few trips up and down the board before you fully commit.

Back to John . . . what response did his actions warrant? Both Doug and John obviously disrupted class, but I see the situations differently. Doug actively subverted what I tried to accomplish. John celebrated, in a way, the disruption to the normal order I myself introduced. But I had to show the students how to act within the disruption. If the teacher introduces an anomaly and the students follow along with anomalies of their own, well, we

____

64   Here Peterson's conception of chaos as a realm where one does not know how to act applies. What I attempted to teach them was theologically correct, but no group of seventh graders can handle anything with the word "homo" in it. I had not prepared them on how to act before introducing the term. I needed to prepare them to venture into a world where such a word might be spoken aloud. https://www.youtube.com/watch?v=GwQW3KW3DCc.

should expect that. The key involves initiating a somersault toward order, and that meant I myself had to join in and laugh.

That wasn't hard. What he did *was* funny.

CHAPTER 16

The Fringe in Play

Having explained some applications for the core and navigating chaos, we now examine the fringe, the boundary between the two.

We begin by looking back at the story of Gus, Bill, and Steve from the first chapter. Previously, I gave no explanation for my actions, but here I will explain (though not necessarily defend) my actions, or lack thereof. Obviously, one would not allow their behavior in the classroom. A teacher's core could not tolerate anything remotely like students shoving each other. Outside, at recess, one would just as obviously not intervene, provided they hurt no one.

The hallways fall in between these two. The classroom is very much the teacher's space. Outside belongs to the students almost entirely. The hallways belong to both students and teachers in a somewhat fluid way. Here teachers should use caution. Classrooms belong to specific teachers, hallways to every teacher, and hence, to no teacher. Thus, sometimes the most zealous teacher "wins" and controls hallways in the name of everyone else. Administrators should note the possibility of this dynamic emerging.

So in general, I hesitate before taking action in fringe spaces. But I had to admit that their shoving each other went too far, even if they intended no harm. Because it happened in the fringe, I gave them a pass on any discipline.

You have to let some things breathe a little.

I stole this phrase from my wife, Linda, who easily ranks as the best leader of student discussions I have seen. Thankfully, various administrators recognize this as well, and every so often she gives some staff training on the topic. She specializes in running different kinds of discussions that function with different dynamics, one of them the "pods" format. Here she divides students up into groups of three to four around the room, and each "pod" has their own discussion about a given topic. Without fail, every time she presents this option, she gets the question, "But how do you assess the students if you cannot hear and observe everything?"

Indeed, one cannot really assess them.[65] That's the whole point. Students obviously know that you cannot grade them with precision, and this creates a different dynamic in the activity.

It might help to envision your class as akin to a bottle of wine with a mixture of different textures, flavors, and so on. With wine, you have to let it breathe a little.

In the fringe, you will assess less accurately because you have less control. This means you will need more generosity in your grading

---

65   Having learned from her, when I do these discussions, I walk around a bit and drop in for a few moments to each pod a few times. If it looks like everyone is more or less engaged, I will give them a small 100 percent grade. So it is likely that students will get good grades on the activity, and this in turn helps many students relax.

of students in the fringe to make up for your lack of information. All of these things are positives, not negatives.

First, we know that grades are artificial. Somehow, somewhere (probably in Germany), a 95 came to mean an *A*. The distinction between *A* and *B* will always contain arbitrary ambiguity. Grades have useful purposes, but they should serve us, not control us. The person, not the curriculum, or a number, remains our constant target. Ultimately, the grade should signal that the student performed well at the tasks we gave them. We often say we want independence and initiative from our students. Sometimes to get this, we have to fight that other voice, the one that seeks control. This may seem counterintuitive, because we need to establish control to form a core. But after creating proper distinctions between space and time, you need to occasionally let them blend together.

Second, we need to avoid too much counting and measuring.[66] We can view God's work in creation as separating and delineating or, in a way, allowing for clear perception and distinction. Of course, this is "good," as Genesis states. But His rest on the seventh day means, in part, leaving things vague and undefined, or allowing for

---

66   A curious dynamic exists in the idea of a census or excessive counting. Note that when we take a census, ostensibly to give those in power more control, the end result is often more political dissension. We see a similar dynamic in the census ordered by King David (2 Sm. 24). Note also that a census preceded the birth of Christ. Rome's seeking for order preceded the coming of the rock that would destroy them (Dan. 2:34–35).

An astute student once asked, however, what about the census taken in the Book of Numbers? This made me pause, and I had no answer for him at that time. Clearly, a census in itself could not be bad but must be wrong at certain times. How to work this out?

Tentatively, I suggest the following: (1) the census in Numbers involved core formation for the nation of Israel and thus was appropriate at that time, and (2) the census in 2 Samuel came at a time when such core actions spoke more to extending power inappropriately. Even the slippery Abner expressed grave concern at David's action. We can assume that David undertook this toward the end of his reign—at its fringe—not a time for consolidating power.

a space teachers do not work over and bring to a specific order.[67] If we pattern our teaching in line with creation itself, our class activities and grading should reflect this as well.[68]

This cuts against our instincts and training. Western education, along with Western civilization as a whole, has arrived at its current moment through intense measurement. We see this with modern science. We live in a world where our power and comforts come from breaking down matter into its smallest constituent parts and then refashioning them at our pleasure. But too much measurement can lead to absurdities removed completely from experience. I recall listening to an interview with a brilliant physicist who argued that choice involved nothing more than an illusion. We can break down what we call "choice" into physical and chemical processes so minute that we have no awareness or control over them. If choice arises from a million different tiny things over which we have no conscious awareness, he argued, we can have nothing called "choice."

The poor man . . . if he stopped looking at a million tiny things and stepped back for a moment to look at his life as a whole, choice would reveal itself rather obviously.

---

67   Philo of Alexandria has this to say about the number seven: *"Such is the holiness inherent by nature in the number seven that it has a singular value in relation to all the numbers within the decade: for some of these engender without being engendered, some are engendered but do not engender, some do both, both engender and are engendered. Seven alone is seen in none of these divisions.*

"The one engenders all the successive numbers, but is engendered by none whatsoever; eight is engendered by twice four, but engenders no number within the decade; four again holds the place of both the father—for it engenders eight and is engendered by twice two. Three begets nine, though has no parent.

"Seven alone is of such a nature to engender or be engendered. It is on this account that philosophers compare the number seven to the virgin and motherless Athena, who is said to have appeared out of the head of Zeus. The Pythagoreans see in Seven both Master and Commander, for it remains unmoved and moves not, the pillar of all others."

68   I am not suggesting that everyone gets an *A* on such activities, though your grading will have to be generous, as already mentioned. I advocate here for teachers to allow for some parts of the gradebook to reflect "impressions."

One can see this same dynamic at play in the nation-state itself, another Western invention of arbitrary measurement. In an interview with Tyler Cowen, the philosopher David Bentley Hart noted that the creation of the nation-state was "always as much an effective history as a flight from history."[69] That is, the nation-state involved increasing our mastery of space, thereby reducing conflict caused by (in one view, at least) meddlesome religious and philosophical ideas. But this imposition of space over the fluidity of time could be achieved only by a flight from nature. Nation-states often unite people not on the basis of shared cultures, beliefs, or experiences but via an arbitrary line on a map. We can see the rise of modern populism as, in part, a reaction against this "flight from history," as Hart defines it.[70] Too much definition of reality and its attendant fragmentation go hand in hand.[71]

Many assume that the most important aspects of life require the highest precision. But this is wrong. The most important aspects of your cosmos, which include your classroom, need a fringe.

---

69   *Conversations with Tyler*, July 12, 2022 episode.

70   One can see the need to artificially impose space, arising from the religious fragmentation of the sixteenth and seventeenth centuries, but one can also go back further than that. Might we see the splintering of the Western church in the Reformation as a result of the excessive "measurement" of the Renaissance? Closer to our own era, Western imperialism has a very mixed historical record. We can say for sure that our drawing of arbitrary, artificial lines on a map led to conflicts in places like Sudan, Rwanda, Iraq, and the Balkans.

71   Jonathan Pageau makes this point in a variety of ways and places, one of them here: https://www.youtube.com/watch?v=qM_kQjpAK6g.

CHAPTER 17

Fringe Practicum: Two Examples

"Mr. Mathwin, you need to press the red button on the left of the screen."

"No, Bobby's wrong, just jiggle the connector thingy, Mr. Mathwin."

"Mr. Mathwin, on the TV remote, there is a button on the upper right. You have to . . ."

"You have to go to the settings function, Mr. Mathwin, and . . ."

Invariably, my least favorite moments of the year come down to two things: (1) the video I want to watch refuses to play, and (2) the medley of voices and instructions that immediately cascade upon me the moment students see the problem.

Actually, that's not quite true. You won't hear anything immediately. After you press play and nothing happens, junior high students grant you about three seconds before you hear their voices. High school students give you about six or seven.

After that, welcome to the jungle.

Showing a video is not the greatest lesson plan, but it occasionally has merit. Videos signal to your students a transition, which inevitably involves a movement into the fringe, a fluid boundary. Many have no doubt experienced a similar chorus of instructional voices in similar circumstances. Let us consider why this happens and how to properly reset your classroom.

First, when you announce that the class will watch a video, students relax and get happier, which leads to talking, mild excitement, etc. Then, you will need to have them tighten up briefly: "Everyone quiet down," etc.

So videos involve first announcing they can "loosen up," then you have to tighten them. This kind of seesaw dynamic will lead to a flood if things go wrong. If things go right and the video plays, they will settle in fine. When YouTube misfires, things quickly move from the fringe (watching a video) into chaos.[72]

Of course, at this point, you could raise your voice, demanding silence. It would probably work after two or three bellows of "Be quiet!"

It would work . . . in a way. It would also feel weird to the students and hopefully to you as well.

I believe you have better options.

First, acknowledge the inevitability of the fringe slipping into chaos in this scenario. The pattern will manifest itself. Avoiding surprise at this eventuality will help you stay focused.

---

72   At times I have attempted to preempt this almost inevitable pattern by announcing in the class the day before that we will see a video tomorrow. This mitigates the extremes of the pattern, but it also involves risk. What if you forget the video? What if you realize before class that you can't watch the video today because you have to move your quiz to Thursday, which means you have to review today? When you promise relaxation and deliver work, prepare for rough sledding.

Sometimes one has to let chaos play itself out. I recommend staying silent as you fiddle with the buttons. You can ignore the voices, which will die out soon enough. In time, they might self-correct and reset themselves. Someone might say, "Guys, be quiet. Mr. Mathwin is working on it," and order soon returns.

If that fails, wait until you have fixed the problem and have *99.9 percent certainty* that when you press play, good things will happen. Then, walk out of the room. Hopefully, students notice that their usual focal point of attention no longer presents itself. They will want that point of attention back in the environment. After waiting maybe five seconds, walk back into the room. You are, in effect, restarting class and rebooting the core. You walk over, press play, and, presto, your students reside within the fringe once more, rescued from chaos.[73]

"My hero!" they will all say.

"Mr. Mathwin, have you noticed how nice the weather is today?"

"Mr. Mathwin, you look tired, like you need a change of scene."

"Have you read the latest science on the benefits of vitamin D, Mr. Mathwin?"

I actually prefer the more direct approach over such obvious hints. "Take us outside, Mr. Mathwin, or we'll sit here with our arms folded and refuse to learn anything."

Ah, the frequent, inevitable, clumsy plea to go outside. Teachers will hear comments like this especially beginning in March, as winter ends and the students yearn to run wild and free. Indeed, sometimes

---

73   I can vouch for this strategy working with junior high and high school students, but I'm not sure that it would work in elementary school.

one must bow to the inevitable and take your class outside, but we should consider how, when, and why you do so.

First, we should acknowledge that going outside means leaving the core and venturing to the fringe. Thus, going outside will always work better if it is *your* idea instead of theirs. Come into the classroom knowing your plan ahead of time. Perhaps you can announce this at the beginning of class or come into class with a visual cue. For me, if I come in with sunglasses (i.e., my "outside glasses"), the students know what to expect. If *they* drag *you* outside, expect the fringe to drift right up to the edge of chaos.[74]

Second, a teacher should always protect their best times to teach, which generally reside in the morning. Taking students out for the last ten minutes of the day, or the last ten minutes before lunch, is much different than at 10:00 a.m.

Third, one needs to realize that any core activity you attempt with the students outside (an essay, a lecture, a discussion, etc.) will get reduced in quality by at least 50 percent. Never quiz students, for example, on what you lectured on outside, and do not expect the same kind of behavior as you would inside. The fringe is not the core.

Fourth, one can use loosening outside as a reward for a bit of extra tightening inside. "If we all focus and get through this exercise, we can go outside for the last ten minutes of class." You can use this motivation for grammar-level activities but not when you want students to ruminate, as in discussions, for example.

---

74   I tell students every year that going outside has to be my idea. After all, if they get me to relent basically against my will, they will get their way, but I will feel weak. Feeling weak, I will lose some respect for myself. In time, the teacher who loses their dignity and self-respect will seek to regain it, probably in quasi-nasty ways. So—students, it will not go well for you if you beg and whine to get your way. This speech has never convinced anybody. Such is the power of "going outside" that they throw all caution and strategy out the window.

Ideally, however, you match the geography of the fringe with a lesson plan that involves the fringe. For example, perhaps you want to review for a test with a game of some kind. Maybe think of an activity involving a basketball or frisbee. Such things will have more resonance outside as opposed to inside. Or perhaps you have the class participate in something that involves plotting, conspiracies, and the like. I have a game, for example, that involves Roman senators trying to stay alive under the reign of Nero. In this case, the goal of spreading out and planning away from the ears of others matches being outside. The advantages of the fringe can create a truly memorable event when you properly match form and function.

CHAPTER 18

Mankind and the Mountain

I hated math in high school. I also stunk at math. But for the most part, I had good math teachers, one of whom was Mr. Jones.

"Don't worry, Mr. Jones," I would say after banging out another *C* on an Algebra test. "It's not you. It's me."

Mr. Jones reassured me. He had no worries.

Mr. Jones had several good qualities. For starters, he had remarkable self-control. Students would ask question after question, sometimes the same question that another student already asked, sometimes questions even *I* knew the answer to, and still he never wavered. He answered every student in the same measured, even tones. I can't recall him ever raising his voice.

He had absolute command over the subject and his students. I had a few upper-level classes in high school, but not this one. My Algebra I class contained a motley assortment. Still, no one ever even thought of trying anything. This was not because he barked at students as he strode about the room. In fact, he sat down at the front for 90 percent of class, doing problems on an overhead projector so he could face us. I would rarely advise anyone to sit at all in class, and yet Mr. Jones pulled it off.[75]

Part of the reason no doubt lay in Mr. Jones's impressive physique. He wore shirts that let people know he worked out but nothing flashy, no "gun shows." He also walked in a particular way that bespoke authority, not unlike John Travolta in *Broken Arrow*.[76] A few daring students, far out of earshot, called him "Robocop."

Each day, Mr. Jones conducted his class in exactly the same manner. Everyone always knew what to expect. First, we would go over homework. He sat us in alphabetical order, and he always started with one of the two sides of the room. With a last name beginning with *M*, I knew I would have to answer somewhere between the eleventh or fifteenth problem, depending on absences and such. I paid special attention to those particular questions, and . . . not as much to the others. After reviewing homework, he gave us the new concepts and answered the attendant student queries. Whether the class asked many or few questions, we invariably finished just at the right moment. I never saw anyone control time so effectively.

But Mr. Jones's approach came with weaknesses.

I already mentioned one of them. He had such a predictable routine that a student could game the homework assignment rather easily, the only possible grift one would think of pulling on such a man.

While Mr. Jones functioned well as a mediator of numbers and formulas, he failed to relate to students as people. In theory, he made

---

75 Teachers need to move to use their presence as a means of directing attention. Mr. Jones, again, was the very rare exception.

76 https://www.youtube.com/watch?v=3YcIulfPzZA.

himself available for tutoring after school from 3:00 to 3:30 a few days a week. In reality, no one I knew ever dreamed of taking him up on this. It was not only or even mainly intimidation at work but the fact that Mr. Jones seemed more like an idea than a person. Though he had huge reserves of patience with questions, he never varied his explanation or tried other methods of solving for *x*. Tutoring, in this sense, seemed pointless. He would just tell you (I assumed, perhaps unfairly) what he had already told you in class.[77]

Finally, he ran his class so "perfectly" that no one moment stood out from another. I remember his method, but I never recall any particular instance of insight, amusement, or wonder. Everything seemed encased in its original packaging, so to speak. In his successful attempt to avoid the flood, he created a small amount of a different kind of chaos, that of the desert.

We can say that Mr. Jones had the strengths and weaknesses of residing at the top of the mountain. He had authority. He contained chaos, or rather, never allowed it to appear. But he gave himself no room to maneuver and had no means of interacting with his cosmos. He could not properly descend to connect with students.

I also had a talented history teacher, Ms. Blake. Ms. Blake presented herself much differently than Mr. Jones. She freely shared aspects of her personality and her beliefs. Her classroom had an energy and dynamism most other teachers lacked. Yes, things could be unpredictable, but also more creative. She showed disdain for teachers who every year, every day, taught in the same way.

She invented several activities for us to engage in, many of them memorable and profitable, including one about World War I

---

77   If you teach math and you notice no one comes to you for help, you likely have a problem. In my observation, students go to math teachers for extra help more than any other class.

diplomacy, another involving the Cuban Missile Crisis, as well as a mock trial where I enjoyed being a defense attorney. She freely gave several days of class to these events and let students more or less make what they wanted from them. That empowered us. I still can recall an intense negotiation between myself (part of the German contingent) and a French delegate over the territories of Alsace and Lorraine. I don't recall what we decided, but I remember feeling very clever. One felt the allure of possibilities in Ms. Blake's class.

These possibilities meant that she assessed differently than many teachers I had. Mr. Jones graded homework occasionally, and other than that, our grades boiled down to the bimonthly tests. Ms. Blake graded us on tests but also essays, presentations, activities, and the like. She gave different students different chances to shine, a tough thing to accomplish with a class of twenty-five. She deserved a lot of credit for this.

But . . . Ms. Blake went too far in the fluid direction. She over-shared certain aspects of her personal life. More problematic, she told us how and when she graded our essays, mentioning that she watched football while doing so. Naturally, if I thought I deserved a better grade than I received, I assumed she didn't read carefully. Worst of all, when an activity started to turn in a direction she felt out of bounds, she would get angry and shut it down. We had no idea what we had done wrong or what lines we had crossed. She ended one big project because we "did not take it seriously enough." Exactly how seriously were we supposed to take it? We had no idea. And if in fact she was right, our grades could have reflected our lack of seriousness.

Some students grew to resent Ms. Blake, as she acted arbitrarily at crucial times. Unfortunately, our mistakes as teachers tend to linger in students' minds far longer than our successes (the same holds for parents as well). Mr. Jones gave us a steady diet of singles up the middle. With Ms. Blake, we had either feast or famine.

One can see that Ms. Blake had all the strengths and weaknesses that come with residing at the bottom of the mountain. She allowed for variety and particularity. She was comfortable with the fringe, and even some chaos, but gave no guidelines for her students within it and took it personally when we strayed outside the boundaries known only in her own mind. She could not bring students up the mountain together. As I have mentioned earlier, if you introduce variety, diversity, etc. through your actions, your students will imitate you. Prepare your students as well as yourself for this eventuality.

Mr. Jones had unity. Ms. Blake diversity. Both have their place, and both need each other. Mr. Jones needed to know how to appropriately loosen, and Ms. Blake to tighten. Another way to say this from a cosmic perspective . . . Mr. Jones needed more allowance for fluidity of time, and Ms. Blake for the stability of space.

To his credit, Mr. Jones definitely communicated that he needed nothing from his students. He did not need our approval, our validation of his life, or our friendship. We knew nothing about his beliefs, likes, or dislikes. He remained remote and fixed in place. Ms. Blake went in the opposite direction. She shared too much, and when we failed to properly understand her, she lashed out, coming too close to us and moving far too much. Such are the drawbacks of predictability and creativity, both good in themselves. But make either quality the master instead of the servant of a more holistic cosmos and you warp reality for your students.

We have seen how these two teachers represent opposite poles of the cosmic mountain. How you teach will depend in large part on your personality. But neither should you seek to find a happy medium and dwell in the middle somewhere. In other words, we will not solve the theological paradox of Christ as both God and man by stating that He is 50 percent of one and 50 percent of the other. Redemptive history points in a different direction.

Teachers should not think of their main job as "getting through the material." This approach makes the students beholden to an abstraction, one they cannot interact with. The "material" cares nothing for them and, in a sense, has nothing to offer them. Of course, a teacher who taught with this priority very likely cares for their students. But the students will see and know that the material comes first.

But neither should teachers rush to the bottom of the mountain, which involves postures such as "The teacher's job is helping the students be comfortable with themselves." Or "The teacher must boost the confidence of every student, and to accomplish this, they must know them well." This implies that students go to school primarily to receive understanding and affirmation. In this view, students would have a great school day if they sat at the bottom of the mountain holding hands and singing "Listen to the Flower People."[78]

The pattern, an icon of Christ Himself, points us toward first descending from your point of authority without abandoning that authority. But you come down only to go back up again, and the teacher has to lead the way. Students should face uncomfortable moments and will face stress and annoyance. Relationships are like that. Students will follow, however, if they sense that beyond even the teacher lies not a grade, not a curriculum, but revelation.[79]

---

78   https://www.youtube.com/watch?v=7-yTWhuK48s.

79   In evaluating teachers, parents and administrators alike should avoid these two poles. "Teacher X gets the students all the way through the biology book." Okay, but at what cost? And to what purpose? "My child feels understood by Teacher Y." Well and good, but how does the teacher use this capital to challenge him?

CHAPTER 19

Play the Man

The mutiny that took place on HMS *Bounty* has passed into history as the "Mutiny on the Bounty." Among the many rebellions on ships in the history of the world, this story has stuck around. Strict materialist historians would likely chalk it up to coincidence, a trick of fate (i.e., it has lasted because someone wrote a book about it, then someone made a movie about it, and then another movie, and so on). I am not a materialist, and so I think that when we see a story linger, it lingers for a reason beyond mere happenstance.

For those unfamiliar with the event, the HMS *Bounty* set sail in 1787 for the South Pacific, commanded by Lt. William Bligh. Their mission involved landing in Tahiti and obtaining breadfruit plants, with the eventual goal of transplanting them to Jamaican soil. On the return trip home, after months of lax living, some of the crew mutinied under First Officer Fletcher Christian. Bligh skillfully navigated his crew in the boat's launch thousands of miles and eventually returned home to England. The resulting trial of the mutineers created a sensation within England, with many various literary and artistic depictions of events in subsequent years.

I believe one reason for the resonance of this mutiny comes from a classic dilemma Bligh brought about through his leadership. Bligh had great skill as a navigator and adhered to the laws that governed a ship at sea. He got everything correct in a technical sense but failed at almost everything that lay in between the lines, so to speak.[80]

We might assume that Bligh punished his men harshly. In fact, the numbers show Bligh as lenient, flogging his men at least 50 percent less than many other captains. Some assume the various pleasures offered by Tahiti cast a spell over the men. But many personal diaries show the vast majority of sailors wanted to leave and get back home to England. To explain the mutiny, we need to look outside of what we might normally expect.

Yes, Bligh punished his men with less severity, but he let them know that he took their offenses personally. He lectured his men, haranguing them about their lack of care for the ship's historic mission. In essence, he humiliated them, bored them, and made the problem about himself.[81]

Many of his crew resented the breadfruit plants, but as a man of the Enlightenment, Bligh eagerly took to the potential scientific benefits of the mission. Of course, the average sailor would care nothing about this. Bligh at times cut water rations for the men but never for the plants. He also used prime real estate on the already crowded ship to house the breadfruits.

––––––––––

80   What follows about Bligh comes from Greg Dening's superb *Mr. Bligh's Bad Language*, a book with much insight and cautionary wisdom for teachers.

81   Brad Pitt's advice to Jonah Hill in this scene from *Moneyball* applies here: https://www.youtube.com/watch?v=fTjhHrcyiQI.

Bligh no doubt had respect for the navy as such, but as an "enlightened" gentleman, he scorned certain naval practices he found barbaric. One such custom was called "dunking," where enlisted men would dare each other to be dropped over the side, with a rope around their leg as their only tether to the ship. Bligh found this cruel, but much evidence exists that the men enjoyed it, as they had their own lingo and economy that surrounded it. Besides this, the voyage offered promotion and glory for the officers, but few enlisted men ever had such opportunities. They earned glory among their fellows through their participation in the ritual. They could reasonably interpret Bligh's forbidding of the ritual as a means of him and the other officers hogging all the glory, allowing none for enlisted men.

We can sum up Bligh's faults in three main ways:

1. He took disobedience personally.

2. He made it clear to his men that he valued abstractions such as science over their well-being.

3. He intruded in areas where he had no direct concern. He had no sense of a proper hierarchy of space.

A naval court acquitted Bligh of wrongdoing. He had not technically violated any naval law. But, in effect, Bligh had severed the connection between himself and his men, or we might say, between heaven and earth. He could not "descend" properly, which meant he could not lead the mission effectively. The ship stayed afloat, the rules remained in place, and still many of the men felt abandoned by Bligh.[82]

---

82 This does not justify the mutiny but explains it. There are times when students do wrong things, and the teacher is not the direct cause but may be an indirect cause. I think this describes Bligh on this voyage.

One year, as a very young teacher, I struck up a good relationship with a senior named Steve. Steve and I had some laughs during the year, and he had shared a few minor confidences with me at times. I felt honored by this and enjoyed it. One day, we lingered after school, and he told me of his scheme to skip school and the various levers he would pull to ensure that neither the school or his parents would find out. We laughed about the plan, made a few *Ocean's Eleven* references, and went our separate ways.

After I got home it hit me that as a teacher, I now had a serious conflict of interest. I wrestled with the dilemma and decided to call a friend of mine who had been teaching for a few years. He told me very clearly, "Dave, you have no reason for confusion. There is no conflict of interest. You get paid to teach, and you have to honor the institution that pays you. You cannot look away from this. Pick up the phone, call Steve, and tell him you would turn him in should he execute his plan."

Hard words but ones I needed to hear. Indeed, my confusion stemmed only from the fact that I had lost perspective and had hunkered down with Steve too far down the mountain. The call to Steve brought pain not only because I knew things would change afterward between Steve and me but also because I deserved the entire blame for it all. Who cares about a senior skipping a day of school in the spring? But me? I was, in theory, a professional, and I lost my way.

The incident told me I needed to learn how to naturally create more separation from students. Some teachers have the opposite problem, but many young teachers struggle with creating distance just as I did. In itself, this is not terrible. Usually the issue boils down to knowing how to maximize your particular strengths and adjust to your weaknesses rather than pining away for strengths you fail to possess.

As teachers, we sometimes lack awareness of our role. We assume, whether we teach algebra, history, or literature, that if we keep good order in the classroom, we can stand aside and watch the students connect with the subject. But algebra, history, literature—these are all abstractions. You, the teacher, on the other hand, are not an abstraction. If students will connect with the subject you teach, it will be *through you* and not via any other means. If we fail to unite heaven and earth in our being and methods, our students will lose the path. They will find school pointless, and they will not be mistaken. This union of heaven and earth forms the whole point of the life, death, resurrection, and ascension of Christ, the whole point of creation, the whole point of the Church itself. If we have no desire to follow this path, what do we have to offer, and why would any student care?

"Let not many of you become teachers." (James 3:1) Very true, but . . . this is the job.

CHAPTER 20

Beauty at Work

Teachers almost always put in hard labor, even bad teachers. Those who fail to put in effort have nowhere to hide. Knowing whether or not all that work truly connects with the students will always involve some mystery. But I hope that if you have read this far, you have a greater understanding of what we truly seek.

As discussed, the artificial nature of our environment presents us with challenges we have to overcome. Whatever we may think of the model of school and the school day, this is our basic template. I have not proposed a revolution from without to change our context but, perhaps, a means to transform it from within. Out of our often sterile environments, we can arrive not just at truth and goodness, but also beauty.

We need to avoid certain false summits to get there.

We need orderly classrooms. You can build nothing without stability. But the mere fact of obedience only preps one for the journey. It is not the destination. If your students follow your instructions, well and good, but having accomplished this, go further.

Every teacher wants success for their students. But even if every student aces your test, it might not mean what you think. What did you teach, and how did they learn? Students can get good at mimicry, if that's what you're after. For sure, take pleasure in your students getting *A*'s, but go further.

Some teachers have deep convictions and want their students to share them. Sometimes these convictions reside right at the core of your class (i.e., "Shakespeare wrote great plays," in literature, or "Euclid was a genius," for geometry). But again, despite the obvious truth of these assertions, the mere fact that you get students to agree with you may not mean what you think. We must consider why they agree and how they arrived at their conclusions. But even with the best teaching methods, we need to go further than getting students to assent to certain beliefs.

We talked in chapter 3 about how we might define beauty and comprehend it through pattern recognition. But we want more than mental awareness. When we read a great story, for example, we ultimately seek not to analyze it but to become part of it. When we see *the* pretty girl, we don't want to just look at her, or think about her; we want to marry her and have a life together. Comprehending beauty involves participation. The same holds for truth and goodness, where mere assent gives us nothing.

Participation in beauty (or most anything else) will put us in relationship with it, and that, in the ultimate sense, means play. Think back to your childhood. When you had a friend come over, you played with them. You enjoyed their company. When you get older, play involves a conversation or a pickup basketball game instead of trucks, dolls, or action figures. If you run your classroom after the patterns in the cosmos, however, you will give them a relationship not so much with you (that is never the main goal) but with a process. A relationship is possible in this sense, for, as we have seen, these patterns are incarnated into the life of Christ and therefore woven into the fabric of creation. When students have that relationship with this embodied process, you will start to see hints of play.

For example, my wife, Linda, teaches *1984* to upperclassmen, and as they read, she has the students play a game involving Thought Police and Outer Party members. About midway through the book, she gives them their assigned roles via small slips of paper, signaling the start of the game. She strongly stresses the absolute necessity of keeping one's role a secret from others. One year, one student named Ben, upon receiving his assignment, tore his paper into bits and stuffed the pieces in his mouth.

He literally swallowed all of it. When that happens, you know something good is afoot.

Some years ago, students in chemistry class showed up early to school. They had worked on constructing molecules during some recent classes. On this particular day, they brought in orange cones, which they put in various places throughout the school. They placed inside the cones model constructs of water molecules, accompanied by *Caution: Wet Floor* signs.

Perhaps not overtly hilarious, but still, not bad.

A few years ago some calculus students asked their teacher to take time out of their week to have a party with cake and ice cream. Nothing particularly unusual about that. But these students . . . they found out the birthday of Morris Kline, author of their textbook, *Calculus: An Intuitive and Physical Approach.* That's what they wanted to celebrate.

Ladies and gentlemen, behold beauty, doing some of her best work.

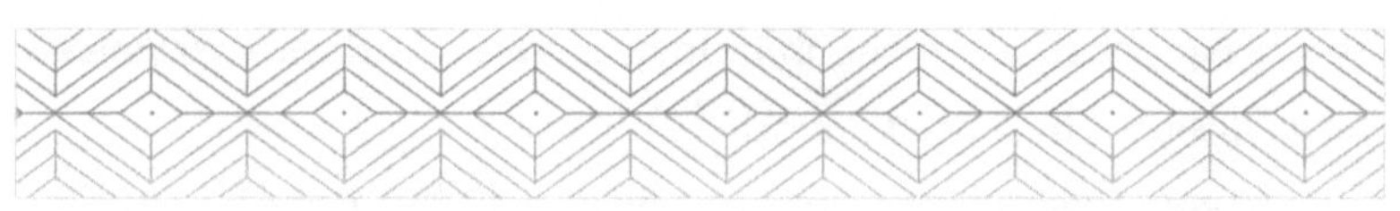

Conclusion

By this point, one could probably deduce that my classroom is not the tightest of ships. For good or ill, my style more resembles that of Ms. Blake rather than Mr. Jones from chapter 18. I actually have very few rules that I consistently enforce, one of them being "No eating in class."

I know. It's not as if I invented the wheel with that rule, but it has the advantage of being obvious and concrete. Students all know this prohibition, and if they try to broach it early in their AFA careers, I break out the raised eyebrow, the cocked head, the slightly flared nostril, and the food goes away.

So lo and behold one day, a junior, Robert, someone I had taught since eighth grade and hence knew perfectly well my stance on such matters, took great joy in eating watermelon in class. Students no doubt get away with sneaking a bite or two of a protein bar with my back turned, but even I couldn't miss this.

And it happened all in the middle of a *crucial* and *immensely fascinating* lesson on Pericles of Athens.

Up goes the eyebrow, out goes the nostril. But Robert kept right on eating. Hmm . . .

"Robert," I remarked with the eerie calm of a James Bond villain,[83] "you are eating in class."

"Yes, Mr. Mathwin . . . yes," he said between bites. "It's watermelon."

"I see that." I confess his audacity made me curious where he might go with this, like a judge in traffic court allowing a guy caught going 90 mph to "explain himself."

Robert, meanwhile, shoved pieces of watermelon in his mouth as he continued. "Mr. Mathwin, this is so good." He took a bite. "It's perfect!" He took another bite. "One of the first of the season."

Now he had me. As a veteran AFA student, he knew of my unbridled passion for certain fruits, namely, blueberries, and . . . watermelon. I have no manners or tact when it comes to blueberries or watermelon.

"Really?" I asked with genuine interest, moving closer. It had been several months since I had partaken of watermelon.

"Absolutely," Robert declared. "Here, Mr. Mathwin, try a piece." He handed me one from his seemingly bottomless bowl (and never stopped shoveling into his own mouth in between talking).

"Well, I better check it out," I mused. "Just to make sure it's all right. Hmm . . . you know, Robert," I continued as the first piece slid down my throat, "I think I need another piece, to make really, really sure that this watermelon won't harm you."

---

83   I have always thought that I would make a great "Number One," provided I didn't actually have to do anything besides sit in a chair and press a few buttons: https://www.youtube.com/watch?v=v7cEnaXU8Ec.

After eating the second piece, Robert had finished his bowl.

I wore a contented, faraway smile. The first watermelon of the season can always transport me. "Thank you, Robert. Thank you very much," I remarked, apparently not noticing Robert had violated a sacred rule and got me to violate it with him.

"You are most welcome, Mr. Mathwin," he remarked, wiping his mouth clean of debris. "Now, I believe you were saying something of note about Pericles?"

I share this story partly because it is a fond memory but mainly to show how one can benefit from this book.

I am definitely not trying to reinforce the "They will only care how much you know when they know how much you care" maxim that teachers love to toss around. Yes, Robert and I "shared a moment," and yes, one could see how I could turn that moment for good with class that day. Nothing like this story would ever have happened in the aforementioned Mr. Jones's class. But I'm sure Mr. Jones cared about his students and would have said he expressed his care by doing his job and teaching algebra. And he was mostly correct in that assessment.

Many young teachers fall prey, just as I did, to thinking students need you as their mentor, guide, guru, or friend. They need you to teach your subject and do your job. To reiterate from previous chapters, Ms. Blake could have used more of Mr. Jones's approach. She alternatively seemed to care more about us, and then suddenly, care much less about us, than did Mr. Jones. "Caring" is a tricky concept. This book has not taught you how to care. Caring brings us near that dangerous territory known as *Dead Poets Society.*

In the above account, one can see that Robert was messing with me, something I deduced when he offered me the watermelon.

Had Robert been eating a Big Mac or potato chips, the story would not have ended the same way. He messed with me playfully, appealing to my legendary weakness.

By now, one might also see this as a means of fighting chaos with chaos to flip a situation back around. By joining in with Robert's violation of the sacred taboo, I could flip the class back to something resembling normal.

All teachers want "real" moments like these, but how to get them, and what might they mean?

This book has not given you a means to escape the artificiality of our modern educational framework but rather to subvert it. Even classroom rules that every teacher has that seem perfectly obvious, such as "No eating in class" are, after all, not quite natural. We eat and talk with each other all the time, at dinner tables, cafes, and restaurants the world over. And yet we all know we cannot allow our students to eat in class (excepting unusual occasions, of course).

Awareness of the real way the world works gives us important tools for this subversion. As we have seen, these patterns of core, fringe, and chaos, as well as the holy mountain, have their roots in creation, scripture, and ultimately in the life of Christ Himself. They are not arbitrary. I didn't invent them, nor am I anywhere close to the first to discover them. These patterns have a reality beyond any of us. We can trust them.

So in ruminating on such patterns:

- Heads of school and principals have a framework through which to think about student and staff life at their institutions.

- Experienced teachers now have a way to enhance and codify their observations over the years.

- New and aspiring teachers have a means to orient themselves in the flood of decisions they need to make about classroom management and curriculum.

- Homeschoolers can have more confidence as they seek to properly order the juggling act between home and academic life.

- Non-teachers can apply this framework to other areas of life and other organizations.

When we live into these patterns and apply them rightly, we can find ourselves carried along by them. Teaching with the grain of space and time throws grease on the gears of the school factory. The job gets a bit lighter, decisions come more easily and with more confidence. A space opens for our relationships with students to get more natural without abandoning proper hierarchy. After all, we find hierarchy everywhere, even in the life of the God Himself. All this can help teachers last longer in the profession and get more enjoyment from it. You will second-guess yourself less, and the job will feel lighter than before.

We must construct order in our classrooms, which serve as a mini cosmos for teachers and students alike. But if that cosmos has any connection to the world as God made it, that order must at times collapse and get remade. We need not fear this. Such things happen to every empire, every nation, and every classroom. Here we can take a lesson from John Huston's classic movie, *The Treasure of the Sierra Madre*. When we have lost everything, sometimes laughter is how we get it back.[84]

---

84   Slight spoiler alert, but the movie is seventy-five years old: https://www.youtube.com/watch?v=RAapNGRfaBI.

ABOUT THE AUTHOR

Over the past twenty-six years, Dave Mathwin has taught classes in history, Bible, film, rhetoric, and literature to junior high and high school students. In addition to teaching, he has served as dean of students since 2011. Before assuming the role of dean, he coached boys and girls basketball for Ad Fontes. To this day, he'd put up his .415 career winning percentage against all comers.

Dave has started transitioning out of full-time teaching and into speaking and mentoring teachers at schools, colleges, and churches, using content from his nationally known inspirational videos such as "Smoke Yourself Thin!" And "Get Confident, Stupid!"[85] Be sure to book Dave for *your* next event today!

Dave has launched *Kalos Consultants*, which focuses on helping schools structure student life in and out of the classroom more in accordance with the patterns of creation. Feel free to contact Dave with any queries at kaloscosultants@gmail.com, and check out his website: kalosconsultants.com.

Many thanks for reading, and Dave would love to hear from you.

---

85   I realized I had gone through the whole book without a Simpsons reference and could not let that stand. https://www.youtube.com/watch?v=Xm1Lzv_wTDQ